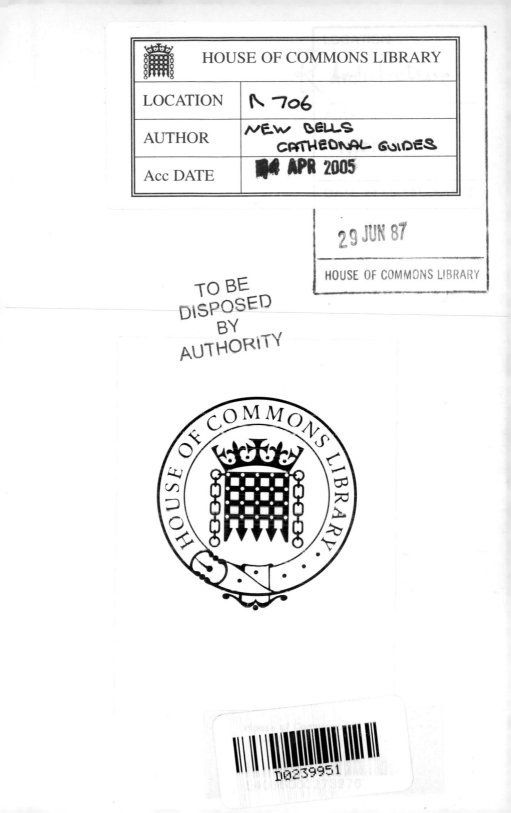

COVENTRY CATHEDRAL

Other titles in this series

Canterbury Cathedral   Reverend Canon D. Ingram Hill

Salisbury Cathedral   Roy Spring

St. Paul's Cathedral   Peter Burman

Wells Cathedral   L. S. Colchester

Westminster Abbey   Christopher Wilson

     Pamela Tudor-Craig

     Richard Gem

     John Physick

Forthcoming titles

Durham Cathedral   Eric Cambridge

Lincoln Cathedral   David Stocker

York Minster   John Hutchinson and David O'Connor

The New Bell's Cathedral Guides

COVENTRY CATHEDRAL

JOHN THOMAS

PHOTOGRAPHY BY PETER BURTON
AND HARLAND WALSHAW

UNWIN HYMAN
LONDON   SYDNEY

For Philip Hywel Thomas
and Kate Heulwen Thomas

First published in Great Britain by
Unwin Hyman, an imprint of Unwin Hyman
Limited 1987

© John Thomas 1987

Photographs © Peter Burton and Harland Walshaw 1987

UNWIN HYMAN
Denmark House, 37–39 Queen Elizabeth Street,
London SE1 2QB

and 40 Museum Street, London WC1A 1LU

ALLEN & UNWIN Australia Pty Ltd
8 Napier Street, North Sydney, NSW 2060, Australia

ALLEN & UNWIN New Zealand Ltd with the Port Nicholson Press,
60 Cambridge Terrace, Wellington, New Zealand

ISBN 0–04–440014–4 (cased)
      0–04–440011–X (limp)

British Library Cataloguing in Publication Data

Thomas, John
    Coventry Cathedral. — (The New Bell's
    cathedral guides)
    1. Coventry Cathedral — Guide-books
    I. Title
    914.24'98   DA690.C75

Designed by Janet Tanner
Typeset by Latimer Trend & Company Ltd
Printed and bound in Great Britain
at the University Press, Cambridge

CONTENTS

Foreword   6

Chapter One: The First Diocese:
Coventry and Lichfield, Lichfield
and Coventry   8

Chapter Two: The Cathedral and Priory Church
of St Mary   26

Chapter Three: The Second Diocese, The Second
Cathedral   39
    The See Re-Founded   39
    The Making of St Michael's   44
    *The Architectural History of
St Michael's*   50

Chapter Four: Destruction and Dilemma   68

Chapter Five: 1947 to 1962   87
    Controversy and Competition   87
    Design and Development   95
    Constructing and Commissioning   108

Chapter Six: A Walk Around Coventry
Cathedral   119
    The Ruins and Exteriors   119
    The New Cathedral's Interior   135

Chapter Seven: Evaluations and Re-evaluations   161
Bishops of the Diocese of
Coventry   181
Provosts and Titular-Provosts of
Coventry Cathedral   181
Bibliography   182
Acknowledgements   183
Glossary   184
Index   188

FOREWORD

THE SIGHT OF GREAT queues of people waiting a long time to see inside a church was indeed a strange sight to behold. This was the scene at Coventry, after the completion of its new cathedral, which, some may be surprised to realize, took place over a quarter of a century ago: Coventry Cathedral is new no more. Time has moved on, the provosts and bishops under whom the cathedral was created are gone, and its architect dead; but more, the ideas and understanding that shape our attitude to church buildings, to architecture, to the environment, and to our whole culture, have transformed and changed, as constantly such things must do. The time is thus surely right to look once again at the church that caused a sensation, as few have, and to try to see this building outside of that moment of novelty and beyond the uncertainty of disparate conviction and confused controversy.

The origins of the cathedral created in the years 1951–62 are far older. The new building is not a successor to that which has been before, but is rather a development of and from an older church, built in the years 1373 to 1500, that only became a cathedral in 1918; and this building itself provides links with an ancient diocese (existing from the end of the eleventh century to 1837) and an ancient cathedral church (founded in the eleventh century, and destroyed in the mid-sixteenth century). This first cathedral and its see were conjoined with that of the older diocese of Lichfield (the successor of Mercia), and were thus linked with the ancient roots of Christianity in the English Midlands. When the third cathedral was under construction, fragments of the first's foundations were unearthed, and permanently exposed beside it, just as the transformed shell of the second constitutes part of the third; the three cathedrals are thus linked physically, as well as by ecclesiastical and historical succession. For this reason, though Coventry still denotes modern cathedral to many, we cannot write of it as we would of those of Liverpool, Guildford, or Clifton.

The churches of Coventry, by Frederic Woodhouse, was published as a uniform volume to Bell's Cathedral Series in 1909. It described what was then known of Coventry's first cathedral, and also the church that (as had recently been decided) would become Coventry's second. Today, much

6

more is known of the first building, and the second—as Woodhouse and his original readers knew it—has gone forever. The approach of this book has been that of seeing Coventry's first cathedral against the background of the unique ecclesiastical institution of which it was a part, and its second as an essential product of its place and time. With the third, an attempt has been made to evaluate it as religious architecture, within the context of our other modern cathedrals and churches, to re-trace, as far as has been possible, the exact events, circumstances, and sources, that produced it. Whether of buildings or background, these chapters proceed chronologically: it is necessary to disentangle time's spider's-web of objects and events that we witness there today. Chapter Six, however, is intended for use when visiting, and guides the viewer to things as they actually are, referenced back to the other chapters.

Evaluation is always difficult, but perhaps more so with this cathedral than others. In general, I have tried to avoid summary judgements resulting from personal likes and dislikes, leaving the reader or visitor free to his own assessment.

The cathedral that was to be re-created after 1940 was from the first the subject of debate, controversy and dissent, as seen in Nikolaus Pevsner's article of January 1951 (the year of the eventual cathedral competition); at precisely this time, the present author was born, and when the final product was consecrated, had reached eleven. I refer to this because in any work of re evaluation of such a thing as church architecture, the writer's *generation* is so important. Readers know, as the 1950/51 controversies themselves show, that the church-building principles of the generation that created the new Coventry Cathedral are totally different from those of the generations that produced Liverpool Anglican cathedral, Truro, Guildford, or even Liverpool Metropolitan. Principles, theories, and ideas are products of a particular time, and while those who hold them are limited to the era in which they live, their works of architecture and art can perhaps live beyond them.

Chapter One

THE FIRST DIOCESE: COVENTRY AND LICHFIELD, LICHFIELD AND COVENTRY

IN THE GREAT GLASS SCREEN that forms the southern wall of Coventry's twentieth-century cathedral are engraved many figurative designs. One represents a man who stands holding an episcopal crosier in his right hand, and the model of a great church in his left. From its three spires (two, equal, at the front; a greater one set centrally behind) we know that the church is Lichfield Cathedral. The man's name, conjoined with that of Christ's mother, is the dedication of the cathedral he bears. This is the seventh-century bishop Chad, or Ceadda, and it is with him and the age of English Christianity that he represents, that our story must begin, since the story of Coventry's cathedrals is inextricably bound up with Lichfield, right up until modern times. The history of Coventry's Christianity is perhaps more complicated than that of many other places, and in order to explain exactly what its cathedrals were, and what produced them, we have to look at the complexity of institutions, persons, and events that were the medieval church.

A cathedral is simply a church that contains a *cathedra*, the seat or throne of a bishop. As a building, it need not be large, impressive or ancient, nor of any particular form or style. The

St Chad, the seventh-century founder of the see of Lichfield (whose later cathedral he holds), seen here in the southern screen wall of the new cathedral, as engraved by John Hutton.

normal arrangement in Western Christendom was for a bishop (*episcopus*) to administrate a specific ecclesiastical region, his diocese. This was established in England under the Anglo-Saxons, who transformed the ancient British church of the Celts. The Celtic church was independent and irregular in various respects, its organization and customs not always conforming with the Continental pattern. Celtic bishops, unlike others, did not have a fixed specific territory or seat, but worked peripatetically. Under the Anglo-Saxons, the Roman practices were gradually introduced, particularly following the late sixth-century mission of St Augustine of Canterbury from Rome, and fully ratified at the Synod of Whitby in 664. Chad, who had been a pupil of St Aidan at Lindisfarne Abbey, was made Bishop of Mercia in 669. He was not the first bishop to work in Mercia (the diocese traditionally dates its foundation to 656), but he was the first to establish his seat in a fixed place—Lichfield—of which he was the first bishop and founder.

Mercia was a Saxon kingdom that covered the whole of the English Midlands and much of East Anglia, and its diocese, centred at Lichfield, is the one original ecclesiastical territory from which all the later Midlands dioceses were taken. Historically Lichfield was the third most important centre of English Christianity, after Canterbury and York. Though it is in the Province of Canterbury, in the years 787 to 803 it did have its own archbishop, and the idea of re-creating a third metropolitan see or archbishopric, centred on Lichfield, was suggested in recent times. Places as remote as Humberside, the Wirral, the Thames Valley, the Fens, and the Welsh border, were all once in the Diocese of Lichfield, which thus remains the traditional heart of Midlands' Christianity. For his humility, piety, and acts of reconciliation in a deeply divided society, Chad has been called the 'Apostle of the Midlands'; but towards the end of the century in which he lived, the great diocese began its disintegration. Under Bishop Seaxwulf, new dioceses were founded: Hereford in 676, and Worcester in 680. What became Lincoln (in 1072) originated in 678, and it later included the diocese of Leicester, that had existed at this time also. And so the diocese of Lichfield achieved the size and shape that it was to have right up until the Reformation: almost the whole of the modern counties of Staffordshire, Cheshire, and Derbyshire, much of Merseyside, Shropshire, Warwickshire and West Midlands, and, from *c*.923, part of Lancashire.

Until the end of the Anglo-Saxon period, all bishops were bishops of Lichfield only (with the exception of Seaxwulf's brief liaison with Leicester), and they lived in Lichfield, having no other seat. With the Norman conquest this situation was to change. Bishop Peter (1072–1085) was the first Norman bishop, and had been the Conqueror's own chaplain. He attended the Synod of London in 1075, one of several held, as part of the Normans' moves to re-organize the English church on Norman lines. It was a fateful event for Lichfield since it directed that the seats of bishops should be sited in major towns, not villages, as had been the custom under the Anglo-Saxons. Lichfield, then as always much smaller than the principal settlements around it, was now inadequate, and Peter left for the important town of Chester. The episcopal presence in Chester was fleeting, however, since the bishops found themselves unable to co-exist with the Earl of Chester, whose effective status was so much greater. Peter's successor, Robert de Lymesey (1085/7–1117) moved from Chester to Coventry. A predecessor of his at Lichfield, Leofwin (1054–1066), the last Anglo-Saxon bishop, had, before being made bishop, been abbot of Coventry. So in about 1095, de Lymesey secured the abbacy of Coventry for himself, and, still being diocesan bishop, installed a prior to govern the running of the monastery, which had, by this process, ceased to be an abbey and become a cathedral priory. He gained official sanction for his move from Chester, from the Pope, in 1102. Peter and de Lymesey had had a cathedra at Chester though not at the abbey—and so had been bishop of Chester, as well as Lichfield. The title of 'Bishop of Chester' was long retained by the diocese's bishops, but it became more of an honorary title. But the move to Coventry was permanent. So, from the time of Peter's move to Chester, right up until 1836, the bishop never again bore the title of Bishop of Lichfield alone; hence, by a complex process, the diocese of Coventry and Lichfield had emerged, the bishop perpetually retaining seats in both places, until the destruction of the priory, after the Dissolution of the monasteries.

The abbey of Coventry, to which Bishop de Lymesey had moved, had been founded around 1043 by Leofric, Earl of Mercia, and his wife, Countess Godgyfu. It was a house of the Benedictine order. Godgyfu is better known as Godiva, and it is likely that she owned the whole of Coventry (a place possibly 1,000 acres—405 hectares—in size) in her own right.

Coventry, like many Anglo-Saxon settlements, seems to have no Roman origins, despite some Roman finds on the site. The name may refer to the tree of one Cofa, a Saxon invader; but others have suggested a meaning which hints at the presence there of a monastic community of some kind. Certainly it has long been believed that at this spot, beside the River Sherbourne (tributary of the River Avon) the Abbess Osburg founded a nunnery in the late tenth century, a community destroyed by Edric the Dane in 1016 (the Danish invasions interrupted the development of English monasticism very decisively and damagingly, and there were many re-foundations after this). There is no hard evidence for the existence of Osburg's nunnery, yet medieval belief in it in the later medieval period is itself very important, the priory possessing a shrine to Osburg, a vital asset to its well-being. In the 1930s, part of an early cross-shaft was unearthed, and this could have stood beside the nunnery, the buildings of which would almost certainly have been of wood, not stone.

Tradition tells us that Godiva was a woman of considerable piety, a great patroness of the church in Coventry, and especially given to devotion to the Virgin Mary, so *she* is often given credit for the initiative of founding the abbey, rather than Leofric. Whether or not this is true, and whether or not she did own the lands given for the house, Leofric's considerable estates, in Warwickshire and beyond, were given to the foundation as endowments, and in consequence, it became known as an exceedingly wealthy monastery. Monastery-founding did run in Leofric's family, however, since his father Wulfric Spot had founded that at Burton, in 1002.

Today's visitors to Coventry may notice, in the Broadgate, a bronze statue of Godiva, the work of sculptor Sir William Reid Dick (1949). It shows the lady on a horse, entirely naked. It is for this, rather than monastic foundation, that most people know of Godiva, and many must be intrigued by the altogether curious story of Godiva's naturist equitation. The earliest written version of the tale dates from the early thirteenth century. It says that Godiva pleaded with her husband to spare the citizens of Coventry certain taxes, and he dismissed her with the remark that he would only do so if she rode through the town on horseback, without clothes. She did this, her body covered only by her long hair (though not very effectively in Reid Dick's work); the earl had to keep his word. It may be that the legend is what is known as an aetiological

Statue of Godiva by Sir William Reid Dick (1949) in the Broadgate, with the steeple of St Michael's (right), and the spire of Holy Trinity (left), beyond.

tale: a story (originating *after* the event) intended to explain the cause of some noteworthy occurrence. The first books of the Old Testament are full of such tales, and if certain areas of taxation were abolished in early medieval Coventry, the story may have grown up to illustrate graphically the origin of this. In a version of 1569 we learn that citizens were forbidden to look at the lady as she rode, and so, by the seventeenth century, we have the appearance of the person who did look, later dubbed 'Peeping Tom'. The injunction not to look at the naked Godiva, and its breach, may be the result of the prurient moralism of the age of the Puritans. But others have suggested that the whole story is much older than the historical woman herself, and has its source in the pagan rites of ancient British religion. The ride of a naked woman with long hair may be part of a springtime ritual, in which a woman represents the fertility goddess. 'Peeping Tom' may reflect ancient taboo myths, as in Classical mythology and Indian rain-making rituals. Or, 'Peeping Tom' could descend from the sacrificial priest-king, the goddess's consort; the horse could have phallic or sacrificial connotations, or symbolize death.

13

The City of the three spires, from north. They are (left to right): St Michael's, Holy Trinity, and the former Greyfriar's Church (later part of Christ Church).

Godiva died in 1067, ten years after Leofric. They were buried in what may have been separate chapels on the north and south sides of the church they had founded. After 1086, the city was granted to the Earls of Chester. Soon after, as we have seen, Bishop de Lymesey arrived as abbot, and it was under him that the city became divided into the Prior's Half and the Earl's Half, the bishop establishing the church's claims to half the city. This was ratified in the late twelfth century, and it began the division of lands, properties and interests that was to be a source of conflict inside Coventry for many centuries, in one form or another. At first, the Prior's Half was more powerful (Holy Trinity chapel, originating early in the twelfth century, became the parish church for the people of the Prior's Half), but later the Earl's Half wrested supremacy, as the Earl's tenants struggled with the monastic authorities. The Earl's domain (which became the manor of Cheylesmore, part of the manor house of which can still be seen) was acquired, in 1330, by Queen Isabella (widow of Edward II) for her lifetime, and she it was who did much to diminish the power of the prior, in support of the town's burgesses.

We have seen how the diocese of Coventry and Lichfield came into existence, but in order to understand what kind of institution it was, and was to become, we have to look at medieval monasticism, for the church which was Coventry's first cathedral was first and foremost the Priory Church of St Mary. It was thus a monastic cathedral: monastic because it housed a community of a religious order, and a cathedral because the bishop had his seat there (as well as the one at Lichfield, which remained throughout the first diocese).

The first English monasteries, in Mercia and elsewhere, had been rather informal affairs, being originated by the Celtic Christians, and then becoming part of Anglo-Saxon Christianity. Repton, from which Chad's predecessors had worked, and in whose mausoleum several Mercian kings were buried, was one of these. The Celtic church began this system of attaching bishops to monasteries, which survived Norman reforms to produce the monastic-cathedral of the post-Conquest centuries. Then, from the Continent, the great monastic orders of Christendom—Benedictines, Cistercians, and Augustinians—began to arrive. These monks lived permanently in religious houses, as members of a specific order, and strictly bound by a monastic Rule (*regulum*). Monks were dedicated to the work of religion—constant prayer and study, known as the *Opus Dei*, offered within the confines of their monastery. The monks were a large force in medieval Christianity; but in addition to them, there were *secular* (non-monastic) clergy. Secular priests and churches existed to spread the faith in the world (*saeculum*) and secular priests, unlike monks, lived *in* the world. Secular priests occasionally lived in virtual communities, and even under certain rules (many—but not all—took the vow of chastity); but they could own property of their own, while monks could not. Ironically, the monasteries became wealthy (as institutions), while secular establishments were often more impoverished.

Today's visitors to Lichfield might seek for evidence of cloisters and monastic buildings: but there are no such remains, since Lichfield never had any, having never been a monastic cathedral. It has always been a secular foundation, a group of secular canons, under a dean. After the Norman re-organization, the cathedrals existing then (called the Old Foundation) comprised nine seculars (Lincoln and Hereford are examples adjoining Lichfield) and ten monastics (e.g. Worcester). The monastic cathedrals were served by regular canons, monastic canons living under a monastic Rule. Coventry was of this variety, with the exception that it was linked up with a secular foundation (the secular canons of Lichfield), where its bishop had his other seat. It should not be thought that monastic establishments required such a union; the opposite is the case, Coventry and Lichfield being unique (there was the Diocese of Bath and Wells, but the Bishop of Wells had no *cathedra* in Bath Abbey). In the monastic cathedrals (as we have already seen at Coventry) the bishop took precedence (as abbot), and, beneath him, a prior governed the monastery. In addition to the secular cathedral, there was the secular collegiate church. A college means simply a group of people who live together and have a common function or duties, and many churches just had a college of secular priests, but no bishop (nor abbot or prior, of course). There were many of these in the diocese, such as the foundations at Tamworth, Penkridge, and Stafford.

So we have to think of the diocese of Coventry and Lichfield, from the eleventh century to the Dissolution of the monasteries, as a conjunction of a monastic cathedral in one city with a secular one in another. In many ways, this arrangement was a formula for disaster. In addition to Coventry Priory's struggles with townsmen and great landowners, it also found itself in conflict, on very many occasions, with the secular canons of Lichfield Cathedral; often this was over the choice of bishop (who, as we have seen, was the priory's ultimate superior). De Lymesey, on taking control in Coventry, had shown that the bishop could use, and abuse, the monastery for his own ends (he had mistreated the monks, stolen precious metals from the church, and destroyed some monastic buildings). Bishop Hugh de Nunant or Nonant (1184/5–1198/9) had a hatred of monks, and sought to remove them. Soon, the feelings were mutual, and he treated the monks so badly that they injured him in the priory church— his cathedral—and threw him out of the city. De Nunant retaliated by having the monks expelled by order of the king, with whom he had influence. Eventually, however, the Pope restored the monks, and de Nunant repented of his anti-monasticism.

When the chapters (the groups of ruling ecclesiastics) of Coventry and Lichfield disagreed over choice of bishop, a stalemate could often result, and on more than one occasion, the stalemate was broken by the Pope, who himself chose the successor: Bishop de Stavenby (1224–38) was appointed in this way, and Bishop de Weseham (1245–56). Various factors were at work in these rivalries and disputes. It was certainly not always a simple matter of Lichfield versus Coventry. The bishop's domination of Coventry, and of its wealth, was very important, for on this his own status depended. Coventry, it should be remembered, was in most periods a bigger and richer town, and its priory very wealthy, and this, ultimately, is why the title placed 'Coventry' before 'Lichfield'. At times, Lichfield sank so low that the bishops did not bother naming themselves after it; but fortunes ebbed and flowed, and in the mid-thirteenth century, Coventry priory became impoverished, and the Dean of Lichfield was among those who attempted to help it by giving money for the purchase of fresh property. Not all bishops supported Lichfield's canons and opposed the prior, as in 1216, when the bishop supported the prior in a dispute. The two groups of clerics are even known to have quarrelled over the deposition of episcopal remains. In 1183/4, Bishop Pucelle upheld the right of bishops who died in office to be buried in Coventry, if they so chose. In 1223–4, the Lichfield chapter and the Coventry monks struggled to acquire the body of Bishop de Cornhull.

Reference has already been made to the struggles that went on for the control of the city itself. Initially, the city, like so many others, would have been dominated by the priory and ecclesiastical authorities. Early in the fourteenth century, the townspeople began successfully to challenge the prior's rights, which took many forms. Power over trade and commerce was one of them. In 1322 there was a rumour that some people were desiring to kill the prior, and the king, and by means of witchcraft. When Queen Isabella arrived, she began to challenge the power of the prior head-on: property rights, dues, maintenance of law and order, and commerce, were all the subject of disagreement and litigation. In 1345 the townspeople were granted a charter whereby they could elect their own mayor and bailiffs. The dispute between Isabella and Prior William de Dunstable became acrimonious. During one exchange, she accused him and his monks of '. . . homicides, felonies, robberies, trespasses, extortions, oppressions, conspiracies, confederacies, falsities . . .'. In 1355, her victory was complete, the prior having lost all control of the town, his 'Half' being restricted to a small area around the priory precincts. In the fourteenth century also, the priory suffered from the Black Death. There were outbreaks in 1348–9, 1361–2, and 1368–9. In 1349, Prior William Irreys died, and the plague may have killed between a quarter and a third of his monks.

But the priory, and its economic strength, survived such threats and difficulties. One source of funds was the shrine of St Osburg, where a copper and gilt casket held the saint's head. Pilgrims visited the shrine, gave donations, and bought souvenirs in the form of saintly relics. In 1539, the priory was reported to possess the arm of St Augustine, and the ass's jawbone with which Cain killed Abel. Pilgrimage was an important part of popular medieval religion. St Osburg was not quite the crowd-puller that Thomas à Beckett was, and even Lichfield's shrine of St Chad probably commanded more veneration; but it still produced wealth. Despite the economic self-determination that the city had achieved, the priory was still very much bound up with the industries of the citizens. In 1480, the priory's flocks of sheep were so large that the town's wool supply was dependent on them. The prior played host to leaders of other religious houses, and after 1498, the Benedictine general chapter (a kind of annual conference) met alternately at Coventry and Westminster. Many royal parliaments met at the priory, using the Chapter House or the 'Great Chamber'. In the fifteenth century also, there were many royal

The octagonal tower, and spire, of the former Greyfriars church (later part of Christ Church, which was destroyed in 1941). It dates from the mid-fourteenth century.

19

visitors, including Henry VI, Queen Margaret, Edward IV, and Henry VII.

Coventry also had other religious houses. The Greyfriars (Franciscans) were established in about 1234 and the steeple of their church survives (built after 1350). The Whitefriars (Carmelites) came in 1342: their buildings adjoined the city walls, the part which remained after the Dissolution resembling an Elizabethan house. Reference must also be made to Coventry's Carthusian priory or Charterhouse, founded in 1381/2. There were very few of these in England, and Coventry, not surprisingly, had the only one in the diocese.

Towards the end of the medieval period, we see how the diocese's bishops became more and more men of affairs, and often devoted to matters of significance outside the diocese, and outside the Church. While busy with these, the diocese was administered by archdeacons and other officials, while suffragan bishops undertook episcopal duties. Nicholas Close or Cloose was bishop for only three months in 1452; he was a former superintendent of building works at King's College Chapel, Cambridge, a task for which Henry VI rewarded him with a grant of arms. William Smith (1492–6) founded Brasenose College, Oxford, and was one of several bishops at this time who held the office of President of the Council of the Marches and Wales. Bishops had a palace beside their cathedral, and, there being two cathedrals in this diocese, they had two palaces. In addition, the bishop owned a house in London, south of the Strand. His next-door neighbour was the Bishop of Worcester, and others lived nearby. Most bishops owned various manors and manor houses, and several are known for their large country-residences. Our bishop had Eccleshall Castle, near Stafford. This seems to have been a square four-towered building (two towers survive). Of the late thirteenth century, it contained a hall and chapel range, and was surrounded by a moat, crossed by a fourteenth-century bridge. In 1448 Bishop William Booth (1447–50) asked the Pope's permission to get rid of all his properties, in order to retain *just* the palaces at Coventry and Lichfield, and Eccleshall Castle!

In the fifteenth century Coventry was a centre of Lollard activities. The Lollards were a group of Christians, originally inspired by the teachings of John Wycliffe (*c*.1329–84), who denounced many traditional doctrines and practices of the medieval Church, and attacked its moral laxity and corruption. In 1407, Prior Richard Crosby, and the civil authorities, were instructed to arrest preachers who denounced the Catholic faith. The preaching of hermit John Grace resulted in his imprisonment, which led to virtual riots in the city, in the 1420s. Early in the next century, Bishop Blythe (1503–34) attemped to remove Lollardy once and for all. He arrested and tried various people, reported to be Lollards. They all avoided condemnation by denying such beliefs; however, one Joan Warde (or Washbury) refused to accept the doctrine of transubstantiation (that the whole substance of the bread and wine, in the eucharist, is converted into the whole substance of the body and blood of Christ). Blythe condemned her, and she was subsequently burnt in Coventry.

In 1534 parliament passed the Act of Supremacy, by which King Henry VIII became the head of the Church in England, which thereby ceded from Rome. Under Thomas Cromwell, as Vicar General, the process of the sequestration of church wealth and property, and its transfer to the crown, began. The 1536 Act of Suppression brought about the closure of the smaller houses. In October 1537, Wynford, Coventry's penultimate prior, died, and in March 1538, Thomas Camswell was made prior. That year, more monasteries were visited and assessed. 1538 and 1539 saw the closure of England's greatest and most ancient monastic foundations. A certain Humphrey Reynolds devised a scheme for a kind of secular-cum-monastic church, at St Mary's, Coventry, that would preserve spiritual functions only and renounce worldly interests, but it was surely too late for such plans. The bishop, Dr Rowland Lee (1534–43) appealed to Cromwell on behalf of the mayor and aldermen, who saw the destruction as imminent. Lee wrote to Cromwell on 12 January 1539 to spare what he called 'my principal see and head church', saying that the city had need of it, and that it could be made a collegiate church 'as Lichfield'. Versions of the letter vary, but he may have been trying to use the argument that as it was his cathedral—and his diocese and episcopacy were not threatened—the crown had no right to destroy it. At Lee's other cathedral, the shrine of St Chad was destroyed and the saint's body disposed of (fragments are now kept at the Roman Catholic cathedral of St Chad, Birmingham).

On 15 January 1539, Prior Camswell, his sub-prior, and eleven others surrendered to Dr London, the infamous disposer of monastic properties—the same number of monks that had been installed at the foundation by Leofric and Godiva. In July the church still stood, and the mayor appealed to Cromwell that the town had, beside the former priory church, only two other churches, and they were insufficient for the citizens' needs. It is uncertain how long the building lingered, but eventually the commissioners were ordered to '. . . pull down to the ground all the walls of the churches, stepulls, cloysters, fraterys, dorters, chapter howsys . . .'. By the time of the 'Great Survey' of Coventry in 1581, it had gone.

Six great monasteries (including Peterborough, Gloucester, and Oxford) were, in 1541 and 1542, made into cathedrals of new dioceses (these are called the 'New Foundation'); they were re-founded as secular cathedrals. Some very large monastic churches survived as ordinary parish churches (e.g. Tewkesbury), and some were partly destroyed (normally the monastic choir and monastery buildings), the remainder preserved for parochial worship (e.g. Wymondham, Norfolk). The collegiate foundations disappeared when the endowments that had supported them were seized by the crown's commissioners, but generally their churches remained, in whole or part. Coventry's great church thus perished when it could seemingly so easily have been preserved, as so many were, in some other form of institution. It was the only cathedral totally destroyed in England at the Reformation (Bath's uncompleted abbey, linked in name with Wells Cathedral, was very severely damaged at the Dissolution, but restored and completed under Queen Elizabeth I as a parish church). Inside the diocese, the king considered creating a new bishopric and diocese centred on Shrewsbury, but St Werburgh's monastery church at Chester was established (1541), taking with it the north-western portion of the diocese, and part of the diocese of York.

In the later sixteenth century, Coventry suffered a terrible decline. Its population fell from 8,500–9,000 in 1500, to 7,500 or less in 1520, to 6,000 in 1523 (it had had 5,000 taxable adults in 1377). This decline cannot be solely attributed to the priory's destroyers, but it must have contributed to the economic depression, and also damaged the morale and pride of the people, whose city had lost so much that had emanated from the great building and institution that had been at its heart.

In his faith and beliefs, Henry VIII lived and died a Catholic. Under his successor, Edward VI, the church moved towards Protestantism, and the country became filled with Protestant reformers. One such was Laurence Saunders. When the Catholic Queen Mary ascended the throne (1553) he, and others, were burnt in Coventry, and many others perished elsewhere. In the reign of Elizabeth I (1558–1603) Coventry seems to have been notorious for extreme Protestant reformers and Puritans. Just as the Queen's religious *via media* was attacked and threatened by Puritans in parliament, in Coventry it was also under pressure from a civic authority whose leanings were Presbyterian or Reformed. In the 1560s, the ruling council encouraged the destruction of religious images and relics. Church organs were destroyed and paintings whitewashed over. The city secured the services of some 'new ministers' of whose teaching it approved. The mass—which had been restored under Mary—was suppressed, and even the records of St Michael's church were destroyed for supposedly containing elements of Papistry. Some Puritan zealots went to destroy Coventry's ancient cross, but were met by butchers armed with cleavers, the sixteenth-century counterparts of today's more angry architectural conservationists. The city's Puritanism, with its concomitant antipathy to church and crown, culminated, during the Civil War, with the shutting out of Charles I's army in 1642. Coventry's great walls resisted him, and later, the city opened its jails to accommodate royalist prisoners of war, and also ejected Anglican clergy, such as Archdeacon Higgens of Derby. These prisoners were 'sent to Coventry', which is one of the explanations suggested for the city's proverbial connotations of ostracization.

In 1643, the bishops' estates were confiscated and sold up, including Eccleshall and the palace at Coventry. Lichfield was staunchly Royalist and Anglican, and so it was now the turn for *its* cathedral to suffer, which it did more badly than any other during the Civil War. The city was besieged several times, taken and relieved, only to be taken again. The Roundheads subjected the cathedral—a jewel of English Decorated architecture—to vile profanities and sacrilege. Medieval buildings had no more resistance to seventeenth-century gunpowder than to twentieth-century incendiary bombs; in 1646, the great central spire crashed down into the choir. But ultimately, Coventry had this time backed the losing side, Lichfield the winning. The last Bishop of Coventry and Lichfield was Accepted Frewen (1644–60), but he was acceptable only in Magdalen College, Oxford (of which he was President, and in whose chapel he was consecrated) and in Kent, to which, barred from his cathedral and established legitimacy, he retired.

Lichfield Cathedral. This eighteenth-century engraving is reproduced for comparison with the graphic reconstruction of St Mary's (p. 27), which may have been similar to Lichfield, because of their ecclesiastical connection.

If Charles II was the restorer of the Anglican church, the restorer of the see of St Chad was John Hacket (Frewen's successor, bishop 1661–71). Arriving in his diocese, he was welcomed at Coventry by Sir Thomas Norton, and at the Staffordshire border by the schoolmaster of Stafford. When he reached Lichfield, he immediately began the task of rebuilding his only cathedral. Coventry had sided against his Church, his faith, and his king, and he it was who took the new title of his choosing: Bishop of Lichfield and Coventry, one which, it could be said, reflected the reality of the situation. Now Lichfield, so often, before, in Coventry's shadow, returned to (ecclesiastical) pre-eminence, blossomed into a fine Georgian town (with a new episcopal palace of 1687–8), then mellowed into the quintessential English country cathedral city. But Coventry, because of its commercial and industrial adaptability and resilience, began, in these years, its transformation into the prosperous modern industrial city that was to be the centre of a new diocese.

Around 1830, population and government were demanding the reform of a Church that, during the long Augustan slumber of the previous century, had become scandalously wealthy, pastorally incompetent, and largely irrelevant to the industrial society that Britain had become. A few men held all the higher positions, some having several (the Dean of Durham was also Bishop of St Davids). The age of social and political reform had begun, and the Church was seen by many as one of society's chief ills. Most attacks came from the Whigs, but it was Robert Peel's moderate Tory government (January to April 1834) that began what became the Ecclesiastical Commission, a body constituted for the task of removing abuses, injustices, and archaisms within the Church. Cathedrals were seen as hoarders of wealth, and dioceses now bore no relation to the centres of population, the industrial cities, which needed organization for ministries of their own. The cry went up to re-make the diocesan map, and change diocesan boundaries radically. New sees of Ripon and Manchester (the latter once part of Coventry and Lichfield) were demanded; but as no additional bishops were to be allowed to sit in the House of Lords, and a diocesan bishop had the right to sit there, two more would mean the removal of two. Nothing happened, but under the Whig government of Lord Melbourne (from April 1835) the commission and its work was continued. The result was various Acts of Parliament, including the Established Church Act, 1836, which authorized the establishment of Ripon and Manchester (effected in 1836 and 1847 respectively). For a conscientious, dedicated bishop, the old dioceses were often too large (Henry Ryder, the penultimate Bishop of Lichfield and Coventry, was one such (1824–36); with preaching, evangelism and ministry to the poor, he is said to have died of over-work). The commission, with Acts, and Orders in Council, cut here and adjusted there.

Coventry was the centre of an archdeaconry, a fat finger which pointed away from the body of its diocese, and was surrounded by Worcester, Oxford, and Lincoln. To some ecclesiastical reformer, bent on rationalization, it must have appeared as a suitable case for amputation. So, in 1837, Coventry was sent to Worcester, a diocese with which it had absolutely no links, and its first diocese came to an end.

Chapter Two

THE CATHEDRAL
AND PRIORY
CHURCH OF
ST MARY

For TODAY'S VISITORS to Coventry, it is very difficult indeed to envisage the sight that would have greeted them had they been able to arrive around the year 1500. Entering the city on the northern side, they would have seen the church of the Greyfriars, the parish churches of St Michael, and of Holy Trinity, and others; but dwarfing all of these would have been St Mary's, the church of the priory and the cathedral, a building that would have dominated the view of the city from any point around. To determine the exact nature and form of a defunct building is a process fraught with difficulties. At Coventry, great imagination has to be used to picture the former building, and to determine exactly what was built, when, and what form it may have taken.

Our sources of information concerning St Mary's include charters of foundation, documents relating to land and property rights, and civic records (for example the Coventry Leet Book, 1420–1555). Early chroniclers—William of Malmesbury (*c*.1090–1143), Walter of Coventry (writing in the 1290s), and Roger Norbury (fourteenth-century)—provide information in their histories. Another source of information about the monasteries, gathered during the assessment prior to dissolution, is the *Valor Ecclesiasticus* (1535). By the seventeenth century, people had acquired an interest in the ancient history

St Mary's cathedral priory—a graphic reconstruction of how it might have looked at the end of the fifteenth century (from north) also showing St Michael's, Holy Trinity, the spire of the Greyfriar's church, etc.

of England, and a tradition of gentlemanly scholarship was built up, that of the antiquary. One such scholar was Sir William Dugdale, who went to school in Coventry, and wrote the *Antiquities of Warwickshire* (1656), as well as a vast compilation of what was then ascertainable about English monasteries, the *Monasticon Anglicanum* (1655, 1661, 1673). These works are vital for our knowledge of the priory; but Dugdale's interest was in monastic foundations, charters, genealogy and heraldry, rather than architecture. A similar interest was probably behind Thomas Sharp's drawing of the seal of Prior Moyses (1183–9), which we will meet below. Seventeenth-century mapmakers included little sketches of buildings on their maps which are sometimes revealing.

The nineteenth-century Gothic Revival produced an intense scholarly interest in medieval remains that has lasted to our own day, though much of this study was amateur activity of

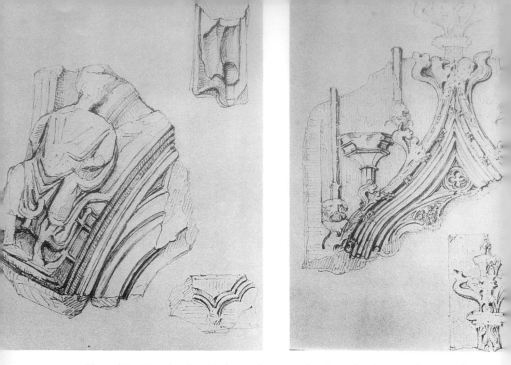

Two of Dr Troughton's mid-nineteenth-century drawings of sculpture and stonework from the priory. LEFT: A fragment similar to the sculpture in this drawing can be seen beside one of the west front's extant pier bases. RIGHT: Fragments of the priory's decorative stonework.

local concern. Early interest of this kind probably produced the *c.*1800 drawing of the priory's north-west tower, in which we see the lower stages of the structure, converted and adapted to form a house. The vicar of Holy Trinity acquired the remains of this, and the south-west tower, in 1655. The northern one he made into his residence, the southern one into his gate-house. The re-building of the Blue Coat School in 1856, near the same site, rediscovered the lower courses of the west wall, and the bases of the same vanished towers. During this 1856 work, many pieces of decorative carved stonework were found, and sketches made by a Dr Troughton at this time still exist today, though the stones have disappeared, and the exact location of their discovery was not recorded. A study was made of the site in 1909 by T. F. Tickner. He found two bases of nave piers, but wrongly considered a fragment of re-used masonry to be part of one of the transept's walls. Also, he thought that the subterranean buildings below Nos. 9 and 10 Priory Row were crypts, such as would most probably have existed under the church: they were in fact later wine-cellars, built with stones

28

from the ruins. A piece of wall found in 1825 on Hill Top, has been considered, in recent studies, to be part of the southern wall of the south transept, thus establishing its length.

After Tickner's Edwardian excavations, no further finds were made until the chance discoveries of 1955, the result of building operations. Then, in the years 1965–7, a thorough study and investigation of the site was carried out by the Department of Field Archaeology of Coventry's Herbert Museum. A full report of the investigations was published by the Department's Keeper, Brian Hobley, in 1971, and the material contained in this must form the basis for further studies.

The church's site and situation may have been determined by the founders' desire to use an already consecrated place (i.e. the possible former nunnery), but certainly it was built at the highest point of the land, a spot which would naturally suggest itself. The church was traditionally oriented, with the altar at the east. The siting of the monastic facilities or conventual buildings to the north, is rather odd, in view of the sharply falling site, and the loss of light caused by the bulk of the church to the south.

No archaeological evidence has been found that establishes the definite existence of the nunnery of St Osburg, and no *in situ* remains exist of the pre-Conquest church (of Godiva and Leofric), or of any domestic structures of Saxon Coventry. This absence of archaeological information shows the thoroughness of later re-building works, and is the result of demolition and destruction.

The church that had its origins in the 1043 foundation, and in which the founders are reported to have been interred, can safely be deduced to have been a large structure in the Norman-Romanesque style. If it did receive the bodies of the founders (i.e. in 1057 and 1067) its building was clearly well advanced before the Conquest. Sources tell us that great wealth was made available to the foundation, and also that it produced a building with valuable adornments that Bishop de Lymesey plundered, around 1100. The building also served as a fortress for Robert Marmion in his struggle with the Earl of Chester (1143), which implies a building of some substance. The drawing of the seal of Prior Moyses (prior 1183–9) shows a large cruciform Norman church, with a large central tower, towers set beside the west end, and towers surrounding the transepts or aisles. Even when we know that such things depict

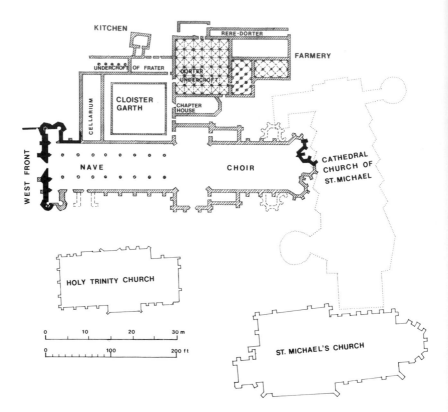

Plan of St Mary's Priory based on studies of the 1950s and 1960s, etc. Dark areas show visible masonry

works greater than any actually erected, it may be that what was depicted represents a scheme for a building that was seriously and realistically projected. In the time of Moyses a church, or part of a church begun in the time of Godiva, very likely did stand, which, still unfinished, may have been intended to take this eventual form. Shortly after Moyses's departure, as we have seen, Bishop de Nunant (1184/5–1198/9) destroyed monastic buildings and began to erect facilities for the secular canons he briefly installed. Documents suggest that at this time the church was 'not finished', which may refer to an abandoned building campaign begun by Moyses, or merely its state before his election. Absence of remains of conventual buildings dating from before the 1180s is explained, if explana tion is needed, by de Nunant's activities, but there is no suggestion of his damaging the church.

A large monastic or cathedral church normally took a very long time to build, though there are notable exceptions. Work usually began at the liturgical east end, and continued westwards. The reason for this was that the high altar, presbytery, monastic choir or canon's chancel (and the shrine, if there was one) would all be at the east, and these facilities would be needed for the offering of the liturgy and other offices, and for the bishop's *cathedra*; these were the reason for the building's existence, and so provision for them would be required long before the nave, transepts, central crossing feature (tower, spire, or both) or the west front. So the building of great churches was an often slow journey from east to west.

So it is possible that a church was begun just before the Conquest, and worked westwards throughout the later eleventh and much of the twelfth centuries, the later part possibly under the impetus of Moyses. The possible need for repairs after de Lymesey, and the need to restore the conventual buildings after de Nunant, may have delayed this work.

Taken all together, sources of information suggest much building work in the thirteenth century. Construction of the bishop's palace (successor to a simple house) has been dated to 1224–5. (It stood near to the east of St Michael's church, where Priory Street now is, not far from Epstein's *St Michael and the Devil*; fragments of it lingered, as part of a later dwelling, till the road's construction in 1856–7.) In the second half of the century, work on the church seems to have been resumed, possibly with funds from Henry III (1216–72). On the basis of their design and moulding-profile, the exposed remains of the west front have been dated as work of late in the century. The lower stage of the north-west tower has been determined (from the arcading and corner-turrets depicted in the nineteenth century drawing) as being of this date also. It may be that a new nave and west front were added in the years 1250–1300, replacing Norman work; or it may be that only at this period had the building work reached beyond the transepts, a thirteenth-century nave and western termination being added to an existing Norman east end (and this could have included early thirteenth-century work, beyond the Norman period which ended with the advent of Early English Gothic, c.1180–90). Or, the late thirteenth-century west front could have been added to an existing nave, since no dates have been established for the nave. Dugdale suggests the addition of a chapel of St Clement in the last decade of the thirteenth century, and the first chantry chapels were founded at this time (chantries are small internal private chapels where priests, commissioned by the founder's endowments, constantly prayed for the relief of the founder's soul, presumed to be in Purgatory).

There are also suggestions of more work in the fourteenth century. If a campaign was mounted in this century, it might have been in the time of Prior Irreys (1322–42), when it is known that indulgences (grants of remission of punishment, due in the next life, for earthly sins) were given to those who contributed to building expenses, and money from rents was made over to the fabric funds. Such a campaign was probably halted by the Black Death, which, as we have seen, killed the prior and probably many monks.

In the early fifteenth century we have references to parliaments being held in the 'Great Chamber' (e.g. the so-called 'lack learning' parliament of 1404, and that of 1423), though where in the priory the room was cannot be determined. A document concerned with the foundation of a chantry in 1409 makes reference to altars (or chapels?) of the Virgin Mary (does this refer to a specific Lady Chapel?), St John the Evangelist, St John the Baptist, and the altar to be consecrated 'in our new work'. This causes speculation about the extent and nature of this 'new work', and work done in the first part of the fifteenth century as a whole. A part of the north wall of the choir was found in 1955 containing a window-sill said to be late-Perpendicular in style (from the extant bases, from which mullions would have risen), and hence dated c.1450–1500. Also

The footings of what are thought to be fifteenth-century exedrae, added to St Mary's priory cathedral. The western walls of the modern cathedral rise up above them.

in 1955, when excavations for the western wall of the third cathedral were being dug, the remains of some fifteenth-century foundations were discovered which seem to be part of a group of polygonal chapels that were at the extreme east of the church. This masonry incorporated a re-used fragment of carved stonework (dated by the carving to the fourteenth century). These discoveries have been left visible, by the side of the new cathedral walls, and clearly show portions of two small polygonal exedrae, which together with the nearby north wall fragment and its window (now destroyed) may be parts of the 'new work' referred to in 1409.

One theory for the form and extent of this work is that the existing eastern termination had a *chevet* added to it, at this

33

time. A *chevet* is properly a full semicircle of chapels, clustered together, that radiate around the ambulatory. The visible remains suggest the existence of three chapels, but a *chevet* would involve at least two more, a fourth beside the north wall of the choir, and a fifth in a similar place on the south wall. No evidence of these has been found, and the 1955 fragment of north wall plus window counts against this, as the northern chapel would have been placed just there. But more importantly, a *chevet* is a feature of French gothic architecture, and particularly of the thirteenth century, not the fifteenth. Some *were* erected in England (Westminster Abbey, 1245–60; Tewkesbury Abbey, late thirteenth century), but they are rare, and 1409 is far too late. The Perpendicular window and north wall fragment might suggest a fifteenth-century re-building of the chancel and choir, and this may have been terminated by three small chapels (i.e. the visible foundations); or perhaps the window/wall is part of an eastern chapel of some size (perhaps a Lady Chapel or a shrine to St Osburg?) added to an existing choir, and the three chapels terminated that. Or again, the three could have been simply tacked-on to an earlier eastern termination, and the window/wall could be a small, localized, replacement, caused by some other factor. The choir's principal volume might have terminated in a three-sided, or semi-octagonal volume, as at Lichfield (Lady Chapel, early fourteenth century), and St Michael's.

This attempt to recover the chronology of the church's building suggests that work probably took place in each century from the eleventh to the fifteenth (though we should not think of this as unique to Coventry) in three major stages: the Norman Romanesque campaigns of Godiva, post de Lymesey, and Moyses; the Early English Gothic addition and renewal of 1250–1300; and the possibly Decorated, then Perpendicular Gothic campaign or campaigns from after 1322 (Irreys) to 1409.

By adding together all that was ascertained by the 1955, 1965–7, and other excavations, a reasonable reconstruction of the overall ground-plan can be made, even if few of its parts can be securely dated. The western termination had transeptal projections north and south, as at Wells, on which towers were raised; it is the lower stage of the northern one which is known from the *c.*1800 drawing (opposite, left). The southern tower's base has remains of a spiral staircase—plainly visible to visitors—which led up the tower, like the one by which we ascend

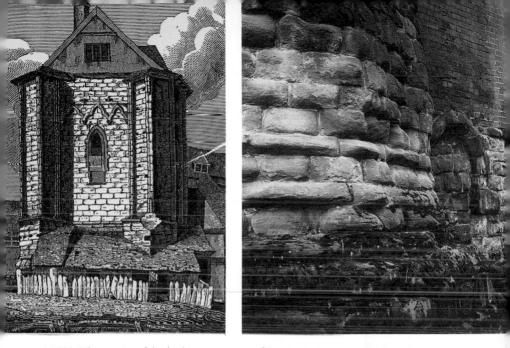

LEFT: *The remains of the south-western tower of St Mary's (engraving dated* c. *1800, from Dugdale's* Monasticon Anglicanum, *1849 ed., v III).*
RIGHT: *The lowest stage of St Mary's north-western tower, which stands in the small courtyard near the junction of Trinity Street and New Buildings.*

St Michael's tower, today. There was a central western door, (and an outer porch was known in 1856), but seemingly no flanking doors, leading from the aisles. The basilican plan normally has two such lesser doors, but several Benedictine churches have only the nave door (Westminster, Chester, Canterbury Cathedral). The foundations of the columns suggest an intercolumniation (the distance between columns) of 22 feet 9 inches or 7 metres. The transepts seem to have been somewhat short in length, possibly due to the site's sharp descent on the north side, requiring massive foundations for a longer transept, and causing room for conventual buildings to be in short supply. Chapels, whose presence is suggested by the documents, may have been to the east of the transepts, flanking the chancel. The Leet Book implies the existence of a southern door, set in the nave, communicating with Holy Trinity's north porch (it was the parish church of the Prior's Half). A prominent porch, around this, like that at Chester Abbey, was suggested in early studies. Excavations made in 1965–7 support the presence of a door, but no porch. The nave walls at this point were about 6 feet/2 metres thick. Some floor tiles, and indications of others, were found in the nave; they had been

35

LEFT: *A cluster of columns which formed one of the westernmost piers of the internal colonnade of St Mary's priory cathedral. This view looks west, and the pier is built up as part of the western wall, which is visible to left.*
RIGHT: *The western termination of St Mary's priory cathedral, looking north. The wall running from foreground to rear is the western wall, the piers were inside the church, of course.*

fixed with mortar laid directly on the bedrock sandstone. The 1965–7 investigations found no carved decorative stones from the cathedral, such as those drawn by Troughton in 1856.

Unfortunately, none of the modern study has given evidence of the internal arrangements of the eastern half of the church: monastic choir, high altar, presbytery, crossing, etc. Two piers, used to support what may have been the municipal water cistern, stood on the site in the mid-seventeenth century. They may have been remnants of the great columns that supported the tower—or whatever—at the crossing. We can only guess the arrangement and siting of the church's liturgical spaces and facilities. Other Benedictine churches of similar size perhaps give clues. We can be certain, however, that the church contained a monastic choir, presbytery (with high altar), and various chapels. It is quite possible that the choir extended to the western extremity of the transepts (i.e. part of it being under the crossing), like Malmesbury (Westminster's

36

choir was even further east). The presbytery would then have been about half-way along the eastern arm. Many Benedictine churches were first built with an eastern arm the extremity of which consisted of apses set side by side (i.e. Norman work); altars were set in them. Many of these were rebuilt (particularly in the thirteenth century) to accommodate a large shrine (as Winchester), and often a Lady Chapel also. Peterborough and Norwich acquired no saint's shrine, and so kept their Norman eastern ends. Unfortunately, we do not know enough about the cult of St Osburg to be able to guess at the arrangements made for it in the building. We have already experienced the difficulties involved in trying to ascertain the architectural development of this part of the church. Some of these post-Norman extensions consisted of semi-circular ambulatories (e.g. Westminster under Henry III), others added a square-ended arrangement (e.g. Winchester, 1320): both enabled pilgrims to process around the shrine without disturbing choir and presbytery. Perhaps Coventry's eastern excedrae suggest the Westminster version, but not necessarily. If the 1409 reference (see p. 32) *was* to a Lady Chapel, it may be taken to imply that it was *not* new, and most Benedictine churches had them long before the fifteenth century. Coventry's foundress had made special devotion to the Virgin, and to her the church was dedicated, which perhaps suggests a prominent, even early, installation of a Lady Chapel; yet some churches so dedicated have considered a further chapel unnecessary.

Of the visual appearance of elevations, volumes and massing, and the architectural characteristics, and character, of the whole church, we can only speculate. Other works, built at the same period as those in which parts of St Mary's may have been built, can help; but to be truly indicative such buildings have to be of comparable scale, ideally of the same monastic order (since each had their idiosyncrasies), subject to the same influences of regional variation, of similar materials, and of similar site conditions and situation—and, all in all, such hypothetical extrapolation is perhaps impossible. Only with the western termination are we on vaguely safe ground: it might have had a form similar to that of Salisbury, or the later thirteenth-century work at Lincoln. As the western and eastern extents have been fixed, at least we have the overall length: approximately 425 feet/129·5 metres. An idea of how this compares with other cathedrals and monastic churches can be gained by placing this beside the following approximate lengths: Winchester: 560 feet/170 metres, Canterbury Cathedral: 530 feet/161 metres, Peterborough: 465 feet/141 metres, Lichfield: 390 feet/118 metres, Chester: 370 feet/112 metres, Carlisle: 235 feet/72 metres, St Asaph: 205 feet/62 metres.

The monastic buildings were also investigated in 1965–7. As we have seen, these were sited to the north of the church, which is unusual for Benedictine monasteries, though there are other examples, including Chester. The falling site, to the north of the church, caused the raising of many of the buildings on large vaulted sub-structures, and this factor possibly accounts for the unusual square shape of the *dorter* (monk's dormitory). Other buildings included the *cloister*, *frater* (monk's refectory), *farmery* (infirmary), *rere-dorter* (sanitary facilities), an obliquely-sited kitchen, and *cellarium* (provisions' store-house). The Chapter House, where the daily business of the priory was conducted, was rectangular in plan, with a three-sided apse, like Lichfield's Lady Chapel, and that of St Michael's church (see p. 57).

The stonework found in the 1956–7 excavations was examined, and it was established that the priory was essentially built of Enville or Corley sandstone, quarried not far from the actual site. Also, a softer, more easily-worked light grey sandstone was used for internal work and decorative carving; there were roofing slates of Stockingford shale.

Chapter Three

THE SECOND DIOCESE, THE SECOND CATHEDRAL

THE SEE RE-FOUNDED

THE 1836 ACT OF PARLIAMENT, which separated the archdeaconry of Coventry from Lichfield and attached it to Worcester, was effected in 1837. This effective ecclesiastical demotion was an affront to the pride of the ancient city, which churchmen clearly resented. Above all, like so much centralized 'rational planning' it did not work as an administrative arrangement, since Worcester diocese was now unmanageable. The Archdeaconry of Coventry (then consisting of four deaneries, Arden, Coventry, Marton and Stoneleigh) was a far-flung province of a diocese which simply had no community of interest with it. The West Midlands of 1836 was a very different place from that where the medieval, or post-Reformation, dioceses were formed. Between the time of the last Bishop of Coventry and Lichfield (Frewen, translated to York in 1660) and the last Bishop of Lichfield and Coventry (Butler, 1836–43), it had been transformed by the Industrial Revolution. In the days of Coventry's ancient diocese, Birmingham was insignificant; but by 1836, it had dwarfed all, and effectively separated Coventry from such places as Worcester, economically, demographically, and in terms of communications.

We have seen how the changes being made by the Ecclesiastical Commission included matters relating to dioceses and bishoprics, and this from a desire to re-locate sees in the light of the new industrial centres. The foundation of Manchester diocese (1847) has been referred to, and others were proposed. Coventry, though in the shadow of Birmingham (the latter still part of Coventry archdeaconry, and therefore the diocese of Worcester) was a major and expanding industrial city, and its citizens began to promote the idea of a new see of Coventry or at least the removal of the generally unpopular Worcester connection. In 1860 this thinking produced an appeal, made by Lord Leigh and W. S. Dugdale, to the Prime Minister, Palmerston, asking for a bishop to be appointed to Coventry; the clergy sent a similar appeal. All was in vain. Then, dioceses of St Albans and Truro were created (both 1877); Liverpool followed (1880). In the 1880s, Dr Henry Philpott, Bishop of Worcester, proposed a diocese based on Birmingham, the largest centre of population in his diocese. He was sympathetic to Coventry's wishes, but the people of Birmingham were also pressing their demands for a bishopric. His scheme was to include Coventry, in a diocese of 'Birmingham and Coventry'. Coventry was naturally against this, preferring to be re-united with its ancient partner Lichfield, than to become second-fiddle to the upstart Second City. But because of its industrial developments, size, and position, the ancient diocese of Coventry and Lichfield had perhaps ceased to be a physical unity also. Bishop Philpott's scheme failed to materialize, but his successor, J. J. S. Perowne, experimented with a suffragan bishop, and appointed Dr Bowlby, rector of Birmingham's eighteenth-century parish church of St Philip's, who was called 'Bishop of Coventry'. Coventry must have considered itself fated to odd ecclesiastical arrangements, since this bishop-of-Coventry-in-Birmingham was almost as singular and curious as the old Coventry and Lichfield, Lichfield and Coventry had been. Philpott and Perowne had both been seeking to lighten Worcester's administrative load, giving some of it to the large cities where it belonged. Neither Coventry nor Birmingham was satisfied by Perowne's suffraganship and the second suffragan, E. A. Knox, remarked on the totally different atmosphere of the two places, suggesting the impossibility of compatibility and united leadership. In 1892, an archdeaconry of Birmingham was created from that of Coventry: five rural deaneries out of the fourteen in Coventry Archdeaconry since 1859, went to form the new archdeaconry.

Charles Gore, arguably one of the greatest Anglican leaders

of his age, accepted the bishopric of Worcester in 1902. He immediately found the diocese's administration and management impossible; Gore had personally always felt drawn to the ministry to the urban masses, and the need to avoid, wherever possible, the old-country-town Anglicanism, that Worcester probably represented (and Coventry too, if we believe the words of E. A. Knox). In 1903, Knox was promoted to the see of Manchester, and Gore used the opportunity to leave the suffraganship vacant and create his desired diocese of Birmingham. Joseph Chamberlain, Birmingham's renowned statesman, supported the necessary Bill through Parliament, and the diocese was constituted, consisting of the recently-created Birmingham archdeaconry. Gore became its first bishop in March 1905. His pro-cathedral was Thomas Archer's St Philip's (1711–25), whose shallow chancel had been conveniently lengthened in 1883–4 by the versatile J. A. Chatwin, making it more able to perform its new function. It seems odd that Birmingham's city fathers, proud and wealthy, settled for Archer's English Baroque church, which, though fine and rare, was small, and not even possessed of ancient associations. Did they not desire a great monument to rise up and ornament their city? Even Truro had managed it, in the years since 1880, to splendid civic and religious effect, and in 1904, Liverpool had embarked on the greatest of all modern church-building ventures, and her cathedral had already begun to rise. Also in 1905, Southwark's Anglican diocese was founded.

Coventry had now lost part of its archdeaconry, its suffragan bishopric, and was even further separated from its cathedral by the presence of another diocese virtually in between. Gore's work had made it certain that Coventry would become a diocese, but there was to be no rapid action, as at Birmingham. Under Gore's successor at Worcester, H. W. Yeatman-Biggs, St Michael's church was constituted as a collegiate church, in 1908. The college of clergy (or chapter) included the bishop as dean, the vicar as sub-dean, precentor, ten priest canons, seven lay canons, and a chapter clerk. The collegiate church was thereby virtually constituted a pro-cathedral, its college formed on the model of the one constituted at Southwark. At this time, some referred to the future diocese as the 'proposed Diocese of Warwickshire' (it became Coventry, of course, few dioceses not being named after a city where the bishop had his seat). In 1910, No. 13 Priory Row was bought to provide a Chapter House for the cathedral chapter that had

RESTITUTOR IDEM ET PRI...

...O COTT YEATMAN BIGGS FIRST...

The effigy of H. W. Yeatman-Biggs, first bishop of Coventry, the work of Hamo Thornycroft, unveiled in 1925, and repaired in the 1950s.

been created, and in 1913, an appeal was made for money. This appeal, and the whole venture, was hit by the coming of war. Chelmsford, Sheffield, and St Edmundsbury had just been organized in time, each being established in 1914. Yeatman-Biggs continued his support, and after the war, the Bishoprics of Bradford and Coventry Act, 1918, was passed. As with Birmingham, the bishop of the parent-see became first bishop of the new one, and St Michael's became his cathedral. The diocese included the remaining archdeaconry of Coventry (nine deaneries) and part of the archdeaconry of Warwick (a total of thirteen deaneries, sixteen after 1963); it thus constituted the whole of Warwickshire (as it was then) except that which had gone to Birmingham. After the local government re-organization of 1974, the city, and part of the diocese, was within the county of West Midlands, itself abolished in turn, in 1986.

In 1922, Bishop Yeatman-Biggs died; the sub-dean and archdeacon died in the same year. The first era of Coventry's new see thus came to an end. The second bishop, C. Lisle Carr, considered that the establishment of the chapter had not been done correctly, and as required by the original Act of Parliament. The first bishop had taken the position of dean, established in 1908, and Yeatman-Biggs's governance had reputedly been an authoritarian one. In 1924, the second bishop produced a new, provisional, constitution, which was ratified in the Cathedral Measures of 1931 and 1934. The bishop ceased to be dean, and in place of a dean, the post of provost was eventually introduced; there was also provision for two archdeacons, up to four residentiary canons, up to four canons theologian, and up to fifteen honorary-canons. Coventry became a 'parish church-cathedral', as most modern creations are. In the Middle Ages, dioceses were given extra-parochial status in that they were not parish churches, but geographically within some other parish, which had its own parish church. Thus, in any ancient cathedral city, there is always a parish church for each parish of the city, the cathedral being an extra church, normally with no parish. This situation was continued after the Reformation by the Church of England.

One of the complaints against cathedrals made by the ecclesiastical reformers in the mid-nineteenth century involved this extra-parochial status. Some hoped to abolish it, giving them parochial responsibilities, in addition to their existing functions. It is perhaps because of these objections that the modern parish church-cathedral was created, or because most of them, like Coventry, were created out of a major existing parish church, which was elevated. This kind of cathedral has a provost instead of a dean, the office of provost being rather different, as he retains the office of vicar/rector of his church (in the years 1908 to 1937, the office of provost was preceded by that of sub-dean and titular-provost). Wakefield, Portsmouth, Birmingham and Leicester are all cathedrals of this kind: the last of these was created in 1926, and acquired a tiny portion of Warwickshire. In 1930, Lisle Carr became Bishop of Hereford, and was succeeded by M. G. Haigh (bishop 1931–42). C. E. Morton was the first sub-dean to become titular-provost, and he was succeeded by Richard Thomas Howard in 1933. The 1947 report of the Harlech Commission suggested the abolition of St Michael's parish, and while this did not happen *de jure*, the old parish was decreased to minimal size. On 20 December 1967, a new constitution was established by which the provost is chairman of a Cathedral Council, and the chapter consists of precentor, canons theologian, resident canons, honorary canons, and chapter clerk.

THE MAKING OF ST MICHAEL'S

The church that became Coventry's second cathedral, in 1918, was one of the greatest of England's parish churches. The history of St Michael's begins in the Norman period; it was, as we have seen, one of two secular churches, Holy Trinity being the parish church of the 'Prior's Half' of Coventry, and used by the priory's tenants, St Michael's the church of the 'Earl's Half', and used by the earl's tenants. At first, though, they were both simply chapels. In this early period, we have noted, the priory and the prior were the greater power in the city, and later, the civic authorities came to pre-eminence. St Michael's may have been established by 1113; at this time, Holy Trinity is known to have been in existence, and may be the older of the two. Though it was the Earl's Half chapel, in the middle of the twelfth century Earl Ranulph II of Chester restored the rights over St Michael's to the prior (the charter made to this effect provides the first reference, by name, to St Michael's). This was confirmed by Ranulph's son Hugh, and by Bishop Pucelle in 1183–4. This does not mean that St Michael's ceased to be in the Earl's Half, or the chapel of the earl's tenants; it simply means that the priory had acquired rights to tithes and revenues, and ecclesiastical jurisdictions, including appointment of clergy.

These privileges were subject to various disputes. Under Bishop de Nunant, the church (and all else) was fully secularized, and though his successor, de Muschamp, was ordered to restore the priory's rights, the dispute dragged on. Appeals were made to Pope Honorius, and then to Pope Gregory IX, and in the 1240s, the matter became linked to struggles over the election of a new bishop. The king became involved at this time, by preventing the secular clergy from appointing a priest to St Michael's, in the absence of a bishop. The king supported the appointment of a man favoured by the priory. When a bishop was appointed, he, Roger de Weseham, tried to remove the cleric from the church, but ultimately failed, and accepted the priory's rights over St Michael's. The priory's right of clerical appointment was recognized by the Pope in 1399, and existed till the Dissolution, whence it passed to the Crown, which held it until 1907. The establishment of the position of a vicar—the clergyman who serves in the place of a rector (or monastic priest, perhaps, in this case)—was undertaken in

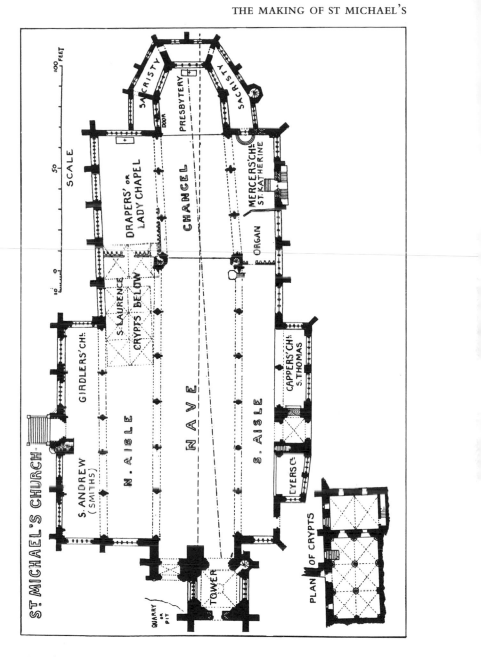

Plan of St Michael's as it was early in this century, but showing the chapels of the medieval guilds (based on that in Frederick Woodhouse's Churches of Coventry, Bell *1909).*

45

1249; at this time, it ceased to be the Earl's chapel and was first referred to as church.

The twelfth-century church building of St Michael was extended in the thirteenth century, but it was in the period 1373–1500 that the great Perpendicular Gothic-style building was created, replacing most of the previous work, and this is the church that existed till 1940, its tower and spire, and outer walls, standing today. This church was a direct product and expression of Coventry's golden age, the time of its greatest wealth and importance. The effects of these influences are seen not only in the church's great size and splendour, but also in its internal form and functional provisions. In order to understand St Michael's as a building, and as a church, we have first to look at the society and institutions that made it, just as in attempting to understand St Mary's, it was necessary to examine the constitution of the see, and of the monastic foundation.

The life-blood of Coventry was industry and trade, and particularly the trades related to cloth. In the twelfth and thirteenth centuries, deeds recording occupations show the predominance of woollen trades, and also leather and fur trades. In the fifteenth and early sixteenth centuries, between a quarter and a third of all tradesmen worked with wool or cloth, either in spinning and weaving, or finishing processes (fulling, dyeing, shearing, etc.), and there were tailors. Coventry was for long proverbially famous for its blue dye, produced from woad, and the many dyers (like the priory) had their workshops by the river. There were influential drapers, and tanners were much in evidence after 1457. Cap-making was an important industry, and the cappers rose to great prominence in the city. Most of this trade and commerce was in the hands of the merchants, who, with the landowners, formed the highest tier of society. They it was who bought the wool, had it spun, carded, woven, dyed, fulled and sheared, and then organized the selling and exporting. Dyers were often merchants of substance in their own right. Of the ninety-four mayors in the years 1420–1547, fifty-seven were wool-merchants or drapers. As in any rich trading city, dynasties were founded, with families rising from virtual peasantry to the status of great merchants in three or four generations. Such families included the Braytofts, Bradmeadows, Botoners, Wildgrices and Onleys.

The trades and tradesmen were controlled and organized by

that collection of institutions that were so important to the late-medieval world, the guilds. Each trade or craft had its guild which regulated what we would call conditions of service, acted as a members' benevolence society, and controlled access to membership of the trade. Guilds were also concerned with matters of production and quality. Coventry's guilds probably go back to the twelfth century, but in the mid-fourteenth century, we have the founding of the merchant guild of St Mary (1340), the guild of St John the Baptist (1342), that of St Katherine (1343), and Holy Trinity (1364). In 1392, these joined to form the all-important Trinity Guild. Because of Coventry's trade, merchants across the seas (e.g. Dublin) were members of the guild. The capper's guild flourished in the late fifteenth and sixteenth centuries. Lesser guilds represented less important crafts, and journeymen. The guilds, being part of medieval society, had religious functions, and were often religious confraternities. They had their own chapel, and appointed a priest therein to pray for their members, and say masses for the relief of the souls of their dead. The guild chapels were set up in portions of the parish churches, and as Coventry had many trades and many guilds, it needed many guild chapels, and therefore large churches; but its wealthy merchants had the money to build such churches. The guilds conducted business in their chapels (some had adjacent meeting-rooms), or in such places as the draper's hall, or guildhalls. Coventry is fortunate to possess St Mary's Hall, which the guild of St Mary began building in the 1340s. The present structure dates from just after the 1392 unification. It is one of a handful of surviving guildhalls in England (others are at York and Norwich). The centre of its collection of rooms is a large common-hall. Linked to the fine City Hall of 1912–20 (by Garrett and Simister of Birmingham), it is now part of the municipal buildings.

The richly-carved gothic chair in St Mary's Hall seats two persons, representing the inter-dependent authorities of guild merchant and municipality. The emergence of the civic authorities came in the mid-fourteenth century. In 1345, the earl's tenants were given the right to appoint a mayor, as we have seen, and municipal government came into being. It was administered by the Court Leet, which had judicial, and many other functions. Although the guilds determined the ordering of trades, their ordinances were approved and authorized by the Leet. Members of the merchant families were active as Leet jurors, and as mayors, and, of course, in the guilds. Coventry's status in the later-fifteenth century is seen in its acquisition of a royal charter (1451) which separated it, administratively, from Warwickshire, creating the 'county of the city'. It was renowned for its great walls, begun in the mid-fourteenth century, and taking over forty years to build. They had as many as twelve gates, and covered nearly 3 miles/4.82 km. These walls kept Charles I out in 1642. Fragments of the wall can still be seen, including the Cook Street gate. Coventry was one of five cities which had its own mint, from about 1469. It existed till at least 1669, and mainly produced half-pennies.

Just beyond the outer (western) edge of Coventry's 1960s shopping precinct, we find two rows of buildings that perhaps give some insight into the physical environment in which late-medieval trade and commerce was carried on. This is Spon Street, situated on the old road which led to Lichfield, and the north. It has historic buildings set on either side along its length, many of which are timber-framed. The street has in some measure been recreated using buildings relocated from other parts of the city; but it was, in former times, just such a street, a centre of Coventry's economic life. At the eastern end of the street is the exquisite little church of St John the Baptist, Bablake, founded as a chantry by Queen Isabella, but mostly now consisting of fifteenth-century work. It was the guild-church of the St John the Baptist guild and has fine stone tracery and mouldings. Behind the church is a group of historic buildings founded in the early sixteenth century, Bablake School and Bond's Hospital. These can be viewed externally. Bond's Hospital represents another late-medieval institution, and one that has survived till today, the alms-house. Ford's Hospital, Greyfriar's Lane, is another Coventry alms-house; it was begun in 1509, and its ornate timber-framed buildings (restored after bombing) probably date from 1517.

Coventry is well-known for its medieval religious plays or pageants, plays of the kind often known as 'mystery plays'. Coventry's plays became part of the festival of Corpus Christi (the Thursday after Trinity Sunday). The guilds were responsible for the production and performance, it being another aspect of their religious/civic activity. Only two Coventry cycles survive, one telling the gospel story from the Annunciation up to the Massacre of the Innocents, another proceeding from Jesus's Presentation in the temple to his disputations with the wise men in the temple. The first was the responsibility of the shearsmen and tailors, the second, of the weavers. In 1529, when the weavers' guild was in financial difficulty (trade being depressed), their plays were given over to the cappers—who, as a guild, were generally resilient to lean years. Production of plays was a financial strain, but the civic authorities forced the guilds to stage them, because of the prestige involved, and the visitors and trade that they drew in. Influx of visitors, which included royalty, aided the city's economy. Other plays were performed at 'Hocktide' (Monday and Tuesday following the second Sunday after Easter), and another source of visitors was pilgrimage; St Osburg's feast-day was instituted by Bishop John Burghill in 1408. When the Benedictines held their great chapter in the city, and it was flooded with rich ecclesiastics, the city's shopkeepers would try to raise their prices, if the Leet did not act to prevent it.

So this is the world that produced St Michael's church, one having great social, religious and commercial cohesion, one in which there was complete integration of religious observance and all other activities, and where there was no clear distinction between the civic, mercantile and (secular) religious institutions. So when St Michael's great tower and spire was built, it was not a nobleman or king who raised it, and the nave, chancel and aisles were not the work of any kind of prince of the church: for tradition records all these as the doing of various members of the family Botoner, typical Coventry men of wealth, merchants and mayors. It is said that the church once held a brass plate which claimed:

William and Adam built the tower,
   Ann and Mary built the spire,
William and Adam built the church,
   Ann and Mary built the choir.

It may be hard to connect these specific members of the Botoner family with actual building campaigns (William and Adam Botoner were both mayor three times between 1358 and 1385), or to know the part played by Ann and Mary; but this rhyme tells us very clearly about the source of this fourteenth- and fifteenth-century patronage; to the works of these patrons we now must turn.

THE ARCHITECTURAL
HISTORY OF ST MICHAEL'S

In looking at the siting of the priory church, we saw that it was set at the highest point of the land. Holy Trinity was set close to it, on its southern side, and St Michael's was built slightly further south, and east, in the Earl's Half. Early on, buildings were erected on St Michael's southern side.

Most churches dedicated to the Archangel Michael are sited at the summit of high eminences. Michael, not a conventional saint (a historical person, later sanctified), was venerated from early times. In 492–6 there were visions of him at the top of Monte Gargano, in Italy, and subsequently at the summit of other hills (e.g. those off the coasts of France and Cornwall, and Stranberg, Germany); churches dedicated to Michael were then built in these places. Clearly Coventry sits on no more than a pimple on the face of the English Midlands (compare it with Glastonbury Tor, whose St Michael's church survives as just a tower), and Coventry's St Michael's is not even at the top of the hill—all of which is very curious. However, a tradition is reported to the effect that St Michael's Lady Chapel was once called 'the chapel on the hill', so perhaps the site was once thought of in these terms.

The first St Michael's was most probably a small twelfth-century chapel in the Norman style. Detached fragments from it survived till modern times. Studies suggest it was a simple two-room building (nave and chancel); it may have had a round eastern termination. Like St Mary's (and Holy Trinity) St Michael's was oriented to the east. It may be that the width of this early nave is known from the remnants of the later extension of it, which may have been of the same size, namely 15 feet 7 inches/4.75 metres, known from the (extant) mark that this extension left on the east wall of the tower. This extension of the nave was built at some time in the thirteenth century. North and south aisles were built beside it, and probably added to the existing chancel. The (extant) south porch (now the Haigh Memorial Chapel), would have led into the south nave aisle. Stylistically, this porch has been identified as work of late in the century; it has cusped plate tracery within an outer arch, and a groined vault. It is Early English Gothic, and the oldest part of the building. Shortly afterwards (c.1300) a Lady Chapel was added, projecting north of the north nave

LEFT: The Wyley Chapel (the eastern crypt: fourteenth-century); the vault's ribs.
RIGHT: The Chapel of the Cross (the western crypt: early thirteenth-century); the ribs
of the vault descend onto octagonal piers.

aisle, at the east. Beneath it, a crypt was built, three bays long
(i.e. on the lateral axis), and two bays wide. This survived later
rebuilding of the church above, and the 1940 destruction (it is
now the Chapel of the Cross). It has ribbed quadripartite vaults
springing from octagonal piers. Parts of its wall (south and
east) are formed from the natural rock. Extending forwards
(i.e. eastwards) of this, a second chapel was made, some time
later, of one bay long by two wide. Now the Wyley Chapel,
this crypt may replace an earlier charnel-house. Windows
connect it with the larger crypt. The site falls sharply to the east
of this crypt, which may not have been built until the time of
the great re-building. In the first decades of the fourteenth
century, St Michael's consisted of a thirteenth-century nave
with south porch, a northern Lady Chapel, with crypt
beneath, a probably surviving twelfth-century nave and chancel, the latter of which probably had thirteenth-century aisles.

Dugdale recorded an inscription to the effect that the great
tower and spire were begun in 1373, and the tower complete
by the mid-1390s. This tower was clearly built up against the

thirteenth-century nave, and was as wide as the nave itself (the thirteenth-century aisles extending beyond this, on the transverse axis): this can be inferred from the mark or chase on the tower, already referred to, where the thirteenth-century roof was keyed-in to the tower, its apex set centrally across the tower's width. It seems that the tower had risen up to a considerable height—above this nave roof-line—before it was decided to re-build the whole church (see plan on p. 45). This work began at the east, leaving much of the church for long undisturbed, and perhaps in use. From the alignment of the crypts, we know that the twelfth-century chancel was set on an axis that diverged slightly to the north; the new apse—a late fourteenth-century work—was set on approximately the same axis, and the new chancel, when that followed, on a similar axis. But the tower had already been begun on a straight east–west axis, and this must have been that of the thirteenth-century aisle, judging from the position of the contemporary south porch (so perhaps even before this major re-building, the church had its volumes set on two converging axes—but this happened elsewhere, and the cause is generally foundation problems, as with Lichfield Cathedral's axes). In the early-fifteenth century, the spire was completed, and around the middle of the century, the new nave was begun. The rebuilt chancel had been made much wider than its predecessor, but its southern arcade (which separated it from the southern chancel aisle) seems to have been set on the same alignment as the (then existing) nave arcade. When the new nave was built, it was made to fit the width of the new chancel (i.e. much wider than the old nave); however, the southern arcade of this nave was built on the line of that of the previous nave, and connecting with the arcade of the new chancel. In consequence, the northern arcade extended out to encompass the thirteenth-century north nave aisle as well, and so the tower, not being portable, was now off-centre. The new nave roof crudely cut across, and into, the decorative stonework of the tower. It is surely false to suggest that the tower was sited where it was because of foundation problems to its immediate north, since if its builders knew of these, they would hardly have placed one buttress (the north-west) upon the area in question; the factors referred to explain the eventual assymmetry.

From early times, St Michael's seems to have been restricted by the buildings to its south, referred to, (i.e. Bayley Lane, where St Mary's Hall stood), and the same problem existed at its east. So enlargement always involved expansion north-wards: the siting of the thirteenth-century Lady Chapel may be an example of this process, and developments in the next two centuries certainly were. The new north nave aisle encompassed the site of the earlier Lady Chapel, of which only the crypt remained, and was wider than the new south nave aisle. Around the turn of the sixteenth century, even more volume was needed, and a further aisle added, again, to the north. Because the new nave encompassed the earlier north aisle, a wide porch, with lierne vault above, was fitted between the tower and the nave's north arcade, this becoming the principal entrance. Around and below the apse, three sacristies were built, but structures standing close by prevented others being set on the south side.

The great width of the church (130 feet/39.62 metres) and the necessity, within the gothic system, to encompass great lengths of structure, probably caused the totally irregular system of bays and piers. The desire to widen the nave caused an increase in height, and a resulting increase in the width of the bays of the nave arcade. The chancel bays have wide intercolumniations, but the aisle bays, to north and south, are totally incongruous. The nave has six bays (arcade) to six-and-a-half in the aisles. In the outer northern aisle, the arcade columns and outer piers do not match up with those of the nave arcade. The chancel arcades cant off to the north. Discounting the tower and apse, a building whose length is c. 200 feet/60.96 metres has only nine bays. The intention, behind the design of these arcades, may have been a desperate attempt to re-create harmonious proportions. This building history — particularly the commencement of the (western) tower, and then the (eastern) apse, on two axes—displays a certain confu-sion of disparate approaches and conflicting intentions; how-ever, P. B. Chatwin considered that major errors had been made in the setting-out on site. The builders were re-building a church (from its outside) which was still in use.

St Michael's different axes, its assymmetries, its chaotic bay-systems, and its haphazard cumulative addition of volumes, all create what Nikolaus Pevsner called 'the great and undeniably painful anomaly of the church'. Though most irregularities are more visible on plan than within a building, it must be seen that such a church shatters the idea of an ordered, rational architecture, produced by the structural logic of the gothic system of building (as it is sometimes seen), and reinforces the

St Michael's, looking towards the chancel in the late nineteenth century.

old myth—of Picturesque origin—of gothic as the architecture of irregularity, assymmetry, and quite uncivilized disorder. But it will be apparent that the church arrived at the form it did because of the problems of progressive re-building, re-stricted site, and the demands of function, as well as the undoubted disunity of direction, suggested above. The church only seems an impossible shape if we try to conceive of a vast congregation attempting to use the spaces, as in modern worship, with liturgical visibility and audibility. Such a thing was never intended. Firstly, remnants of a stair, and a possible sill-fragment, tell us that the church had a rood loft and rood screen (though no chancel arch), separating chancel and nave. Also, most of the spaces were intended from the first to serve guilds and chantries, so it did not matter where they were sited, how their architecture harmonized with that of the rest, or what shape or size of eventual building they created. In spatial and structural terms, Pevsner's assessment is correct; but ultimately, the 'painful anomaly' is the product of modern ideas about what a church should be like. Our experience of space and symmetry, and our aesthetic perception as a whole, is totally different from that of people living in 1500. The church's functional provisions must be examined further, below.

The style of the church was Perpendicular Gothic from the beginning of the rebuilding, which is early for a parish church. It has large bay-lengths (wide arches), very low-pitched timber roofs, and an accumulation of volumes on the transverse axis (externally, from the north, the appearance is of great *length*), though most Perpendicular churches, as the name suggests, are tall (seemingly narrow) buildings, with soaring vertical members, the emphasis being upward. The church's structural widths probably removed the viability of fine stone vaults, which, as latticed liernes or swirling fans, are among the glories of English Late Gothic architecture.

It is useful to contrast St Michael's with Holy Trinity, which is unlike it in so many ways. Holy Trinity consists of a late-fourteenth century chancel, a nave which is fourteenth-century in origin (with fifteenth-century clerestory), transepts, tower and spire. Most of the extant structure dates from around the 1360s to the 1530s. The tower and spire are 237 feet/72.23 metres high. St Michael's was one long, wide, volume; Holy Trinity is a perfect aisled cruciform. St Michael's tower elevates sheer from the ground to almost 300 feet/91.44 metres: Holy Trinity's is a culmination of the masses through which it rises (nave, chancel, etc.). St Michael's spire rises from an intermediate octagonal prism, surmounting the tower; Holy Trinity's emerges directly from the square tower. St Michael's tower is of the classic Perpendicular design, where each succeeding stage is pierced by a changing pattern of contrasting openings (often increasing in size, to lighten the load), set about with crockets and spirelets, Holy Trinity has that other kind of Late Gothic tower, where uniform openings, flanked by ribs of stone, rise from bottom to top in regular fashion, framing the whole in a kind of grid. Holy Trinity's tower is smaller and less decorated, and the church as a whole is comparatively diminutive; but we should never confuse size with architectural merit. For many, the regularity and harmony of Holy Trinity must have been preferable to the 'painful anomaly' of the larger building. Many prefer a tower which, like St Michael's, seems to actually emerge from the ground, on firm, solid walls. Because it is a crossing-feature, Holy Trinity's descends onto four relatively slender piers, its base dissolved into four arches whose mouldings die into one another, intersecting as they disappear, a Late Gothic motif that is not easy to find, but exceedingly beautiful. However, one feature of St Michael's, though gone now, can be appreciated by

looking at the very similar example, erected slightly later, at Holy Trinity. This is the filling of the inner spandrel panels of the nave arcade with a grid of vertical members, which descend from the mullions of the clerestory windows above, right down to the extrados of the principal arches. This idea originated at the Chapter House of St Paul's, London (1330s) and came via Wells, Gloucester, and Sherborne. John Harvey, in his 1978 study of Perpendicular architecture, dates the St Michael's example as early as 1434. Earlier gothic styles had filled this potentially awkward triangular space with cusped tracery, or used the space for sculpture (e.g. Lincoln's angels). These vertical parallel ribs, at St Michael's, may have had the effect of countering the horizontality of the whole.

Holy Trinity's eastern end is a classic English square termination with a large single window; St Michael's, as we have seen, has its presbytery (or 'sanctuary') terminated with a rare three-sided apse, as found at the Priory's Chapter House, and at Lichfield's eastern extremity, its Lady Chapel. Lichfield's Lady Chapel was built around 1320–36, and this polygonal, or semi-octagonal end has been described as an essentially French feature. For whatever reason it was employed at Lichfield, its use at Coventry, about fifty years later, may have been because of the constricted site; but also, it may have presented itself as a means of creating a more varied effect in what—as would presumably have been known when the apse was begun— would otherwise become a very long uniform mass, unbroken by any central feature (as it happened, there was a variation in the Perpendicular styles of chancel and nave, apparent readily in the tracery, now largely gone). Lichfield, and the Chapter House, might have provided precedent; but the canting at St Michael's is slightly different, the sides being set at a more acute angle (i.e. about 112°, internally, to the eastern wall, as against 135° at Lichfield, and most other examples). Externally, one side of St Michael's apse disappears more quickly, to the viewer walking around it; inside, the effect is, if anything, more productive of intimate enclosure than a more normal apse.

A major function of St Michael's, we have seen, was the accommodation of guild chapels. Guilds did come and go, and chapels changed hands, but the major incumbents, and their

OPPOSITE: The octagon stage of St Michael's tower, looking up it, and showing one of the pairs of diverging flying buttresses, which connected it with the square stage, below.

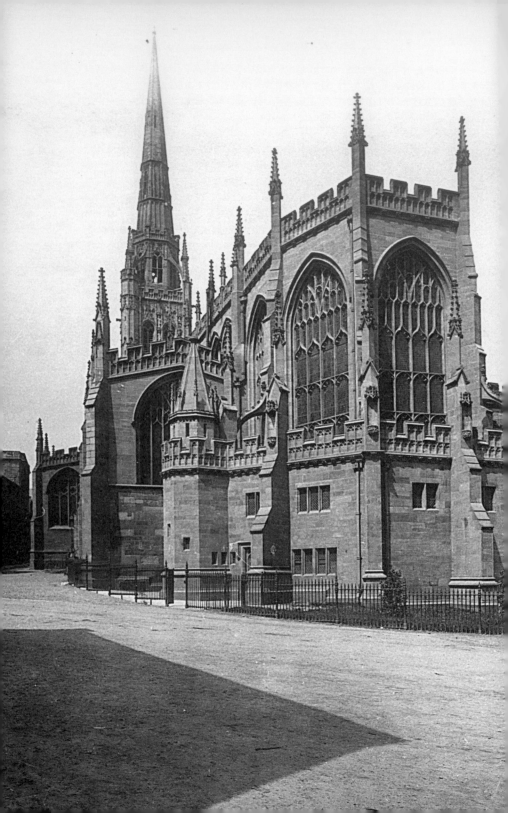

chapels, include the following: the Mercers (chapel dedicated to St Katherine), in the south chancel aisle. This chapel was founded c.1412, and a south door was formed in it in 1750. Much of it was given over to the organ which was installed in 1887. The Drapers (St Mary's chapel), used the north chancel aisle from c.1300 (i.e. before the re-building), and a similar location afterwards. The Girdlers were strongest in the sixteenth century, at the beginning of which their part of the church (eastern end of the northern outer-aisle) was built; they were disbanded in the later seventeenth century. The Smiths (St Andrew's) were located to the west of the Girdlers, in the northern outer-aisle, however, they are known to have had a chapel before this aisle was built, in 1449: they may have shared with another guild. The Capper's chapel (St Thomas) was originally that of the Card-Makers (from 1467). In 1531, the Cappers held it with them jointly, but from 1537, it was given over to the Cappers alone. This chapel (at the eastern end of the southern outer-aisle) had an upper-room where the priest lived. A spiral staircase once gave access to the upper room, from the south porch. The Dyer's chapel (western end of the southern outer-aisle) may also have had an upper room. The Dyer's chapel, and their priest, are known from surviving mid-fifteenth century payment-accounts. Reference to upper-rooms (where business was conducted) and separate entrances, reminds us that the guild chapels were private enclosures, not part of a public space, as we expect of churches today.

We have noted that the chapels acted as guild chantries where deceased members were prayed for; but in addition to these, there were many other personal chantries, established by families and individuals. A St Lawrence chantry was founded in 1330, and in the later building, the eastern part of the north nave aisle was dedicated to this saint (the former Lady Chapel had been partly on this site, and that of the Draper's chapel, the latter of which retained the Marian dedication, we have seen).

Though the aisles were given over to private chapels, and the chancel and presbytery were the separated realm of priests and sacraments, the nave of a medieval church was a very public place, and probably the largest roofed space, for common use, in the town. So throughout the medieval period, ordinary people used the church nave for all kinds of activities

OPPOSITE: St Michael's, from east, after restoration (ie. after 1890). The southern vestry (left) is entirely new.

(there very generally few benches to get in the way). It was used for sanctuary, for eating and drinking, for dancing, playing of games and drama, for public meetings, legal proceedings, and even commercial transactions. We know of many of these uses from the survival of episcopal injunctions aimed at stopping the practices. Cloth was sold in St Michael's porch, as we know from an attempt to stop it in 1455. In the Middle Ages, churches were thought of as places possessed of holiness, and in an ascending hierarchy, the chancel being more holy than the nave, the presbytery the most holy of all (this was after the model of the Jerusalem Temple). The people used the nave (and the porch!) as non-religious spaces; but the church hierarchy saw the whole building and precincts as separate from the world.

One feature of the church which deserves mention is the carved misericords. These were destroyed in 1940, but were well recorded and studied prior to that. Twelve are known, two of which were not given decorative carving. The best known of them was the 'Dance of Death' cycle, which included Death leading a procession of mankind. Associated with this was a depiction of the 'Seven Acts of Mercy' (St Matthew's Gospel, Ch. 25, v. 31–46), and the conjunction of the two has been seen as a reflection of themes in the Coventry religious plays. Other subjects included the sport of bat-fowling, a Last Judgement, and a Jesse Tree. Incidental carvings depicted a legless wyvern, sharks, and a bird-headed woman.

In recent years, exhaustive research had been carried out in an attempt to discover the identities of the various architects, masons, builders and craftsmen who created our medieval churches and cathedrals, and the times and places in which they worked. This study has yielded much fruit; but in the case of Coventry's builders, we still know very little. However, there is a possibility that the designer of St Michael's tower can be identified as Robert Skillyngton or Skelyngton, an architect-mason who worked for John of Gaunt at nearby Kenilworth Castle in the 1390s, and at Leicester, at the end of this decade. This identification was made on the basis of the similarity of moulding-profiles (which tended to be personal, individual, designs) seen at Coventry and Kenilworth; and they are seen, too, at St Mary's, Warwick, in work done in the years 1381–96 (this includes an idiosyncratic open rib-work (or web-less) vault; but the eight diminutive flying-buttress-like ribs, that subtly aid the transition from tower to spire, at St Michael's, is comparable with this Warwick curiosity). However, our knowledge of the tower's mouldings is dependent on the accuracy of late-nineteenth century reconstructions. Building craftsmen who were active in fifteenth-century Coventry included glaziers (e.g. John Thornton, who made the east window of York Minster in 1405), and they must have supplied St Michael's with stained glass.

In 1548, religious guilds, and all chantries, were abolished. The trade guilds survived—though some not for long—but lost their religious functions, and their chapels; often, they sold their church plate and vestments. A 1394 font was removed in 1645, and a brass eagle lectern (of 1559) was sold for thirteen shillings and four-pence (crafty wardens at Holy Trinity cut a slot in their eagle, and used it as a collecting-box, thus preventing its destruction by the Puritans). At about this time, no doubt, the rood and rood screen perished, probably a very fine piece of carving. The church soon began its transformation into a Protestant place of worship, a building in which seeing and hearing the preacher were the requisites of worship and of buildings designed for religion. In the seventeenth and eighteenth centuries, medieval churches were filled up with galleries and box-pews, and wooden panelling hid the stonework. Churches ceased to be a vital part of life as they had been, and many were neglected, and some vilely abused. St Michael's, now an anachronism, decayed, its upkeep a burden to the populace. From the late eighteenth century onwards, the state of the great tower was constantly the cause of alarm. Heavy bells, and their ringing, were often blamed, and the stonework was also badly eroded. In 1792 the church authorities tackled the problem, and in the following January, Joseph Potter of Lichfield became their architect, working in association with James Wyatt, who acted as a kind of consultant. Potter built a wooden frame, which rose from the floor, within the tower, and held the bells. He also blocked up certain openings in the tower, to strengthen it; his work was completed in 1794.

In the 1830s, the tide of taste turned again, and gothic architecture was now valued once again. Almost every medieval building required repair and restoration. One of the most ubiquitous restorers, George Gilbert Scott, was responsible for much clearing of Georgian accretions (galleries, box-pews, etc.) in the years 1851–5, and restoring stonework; his

St Michael's, from north, before the late-nineteenth century restorations. Note the ruinous condition of the tower and apse.

employee J. Drayton-Wyatt was involved in this work. In 1860, wooden panelling in the apse was replaced by dwarf-arcading (the work of James Murray). A fifteenth-century pulpit was removed in 1869. Later in the century, Scott's second son, John Oldrid Scott (1841–1913) was appointed to restore St Michael's under the direction of Coventry citizen George Woodcock (who contributed many thousands to the work) and the vicar, Rev J. Butter. The building's fabric was in a miserable condition of decay because of the nature of the stone. Coventry's cathedrals, like so many others in the west and north Midlands, were built from the so-called 'New Red Sandstones', i.e. sandstones of the Triassic and Permian systems, which were formed between 195 and 280 million years ago. They are found from as far south as Devon right up to Cumbria; many of them weather very badly. Worcester, Lichfield, and Carlisle's cathedrals have suffered terribly, as well as St Michael's, but probably Chester's worst of all.

In his work, Scott used Runcorn stone, which has so far weathered better. In the years 1883–90, he restored the clerestories, chancel, apse, tower and spire. The ruinous eastern end had lost most of its buttresses and some parapets; when these

The under-tower vault of St Michael's, as re-created by J. O. Scott c. 1890.

were replaced the present southern sacristy was added, completing the ring of sacristies (a Georgian vestry, on the site, was removed). Fatefully, Scott put iron tie-rods across the roof-structure (the clerestory walls were probably spreading outwards). The tower was very badly eroded (old photographs show the buttresses simply hanging off) and very little of the original moulding was left upon which Scott could base his reconstructions. However, some thirty-five years before, Drayton-Wyatt had made measured drawings of St Michael's, and Scott used these. The tower was also cracked (it had required further attention from Potter in 1818, and in fact his bell-frame, which Scott now removed, had *added* to the damage). The extent of the quarry, just north of the tower, was now discovered, and precarious underpinning was carried out. A gigantic cage of timber scaffolding was erected around the tower and spire, whose total height was decreased slightly, from about 300 feet/91.44 metres to about 295 feet/89.91 metres. The present under-tower vault was constructed as part of this work, only a few broken stumps of medieval ribs remaining (Frederic Woodhouse claimed that the medieval vault had been destroyed following the re-casting of the bells

SCALE OF ⊢⊢⊢⊢⊢⊢ 10 5 0   10   20   30   40   50 FEET

ABOVE: St Michael's tower and spire, elevation and part-section, 'as about to be restored by J. O. Scott,' from the Building News *14 November 1884.*

OPPOSITE: St Michael's from north west (ie. Holy Trinity's roof) after restoration (ie. post-1890).

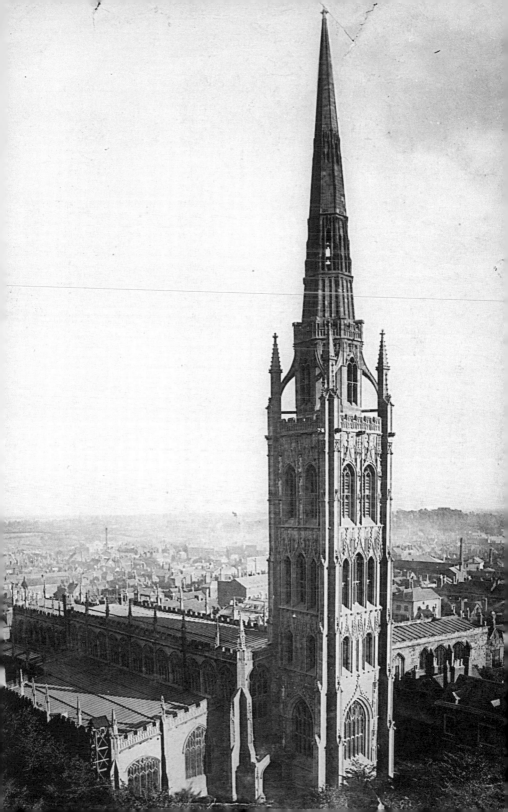

*The cathedral c. 1936, looking west. The arcading and statuary of the chancel are gone;
the altar, and walls beside it, await their final re-furnishing.*

in 1674–5). Many believed the bells to be the source of the
tower's problems, yet naturally few wanted the bells silenced.
Scott agreed that the tower could not support rung bells unaided by some further structural addition. Woodcock opposed
this, and offered half the cost of a free-standing campanile (an
idea suggested as early as 1793). Scott produced a design in
1888, as also did 'Camera Principis' (i.e. George Webster: his
tower was to adjoin the church). In April 1890, the restoration
was officially complete, and a commission of eminent architects met to consider the wisdom of a free-standing campanile.
They approved the idea, and in March 1891, the excellent
northern gothicists, Paley and Austin of Lancaster, produced a
design, a Late Gothic tower, with strong vertical ribwork, like
that of Holy Trinity, to the west of which it was to be sited. In
May, Woodcock suddenly died, and the campanile scheme
died with him. When the church was designated a pro-

cathedral, some feared plans for great extensions, but again, nothing was built.

Sadly, however, the pre-1940 architectural history does not end here. In the mid-1930s, it was decided to re-furnish the sanctuary. The (Victorian) floor-level was lowered, and the altar with it. In addition, however, James Murray's arcading and some statuary were cut out, the walls levelled, whitened, and grimly sanitized, the harmonious decorative richness turned to banality, the whole suggesting the white-tile aesthetics of the municipal convenience. This was presumably the work of cathedral architect W. H. Randoll Blacking (1889–1958) of Salisbury, and was completed in 1937.

Chapter Four

DESTRUCTION AND DILEMMA

IT SEEMS THAT EACH YEAR, in November, the German Führer returned to Munich to celebrate with his 'old comrades', those with whom, in 1923, he had attempted to wrest power from the rulers of the Weimar Republic. But his celebrations and speech of 8 November 1940, were rudely interrupted by a British bombing raid. At this time, Germany was attempting to achieve some kind of treaty with the USSR, by which the two nations would divide power over much of the world, abjuring mutual aggression. Molotov, the Soviet Foreign Minister, arrived in Berlin, to this end, on 12 November. On the following evening at dinner, he toasted his German hosts; but when von Ribbentrop rose to reply, pandemonium broke out. The Royal Air Force had attacked Berlin since August, but this time the planes had arrived especially early, Winston Churchill considering that the British, while not invited to the banquet, should not go unrepresented; the whole gathering was sent ignominiously scuttling to the shelters. It was decided that 'Mr. Churchill's new brain child . . . the night air raid'—as Hitler called it—must now be stopped. Reprisal was necessary. A fitting act was the material and psychological destruction of an entire city. London—for months, now, the target—had proved too large for the Luftwaffe to raze, and besides, as the insults had involved air attack, the target city had to be one engaged in production of war-planes. Such cities were in the Midlands. Birmingham was surely also too large, so the choice was narrowed to Coventry, having about a quarter of a million inhabitants, and many aircraft factories. But how to hit such a relatively small target? Germany had developed the *knickebein* system, involving two radio beams which intersected over the target, and guided the bombers in. But in June 1940, the British had learnt to deflect the beams, with the result that hundreds of high-explosive bombs were seen to fall on empty country fields; no one in Germany dared tell Air Marshall Goering of this for some time. However, a formation known as *Kampfgruppe 100* had a system known as '*X' Gerät*. The British had a jamming device for this also, by mid-September, but a single calculational error made by one scientist, rendered it inoperable for a few months longer. A 'pathfinder' unit was formed from Kampfgruppe 100, who, on the night of Thursday 14 November, located the city with their unassailable system; it was a clear night, with strong moonlight. The 'pathfinders' carried incendiary canisters, the sole purpose of which was to create many large fires so that the following waves of planes could locate the target with the naked eye, unaided; these successors would carry the high-explosive bombs, which were intended to destroy the target.

The authorities had known from the first that the Midland cities were especially vulnerable, Churchill realizing it shortly after Dunkirk. Coventry had been used as a suitable subject for a report made by the Ministry of Home Security, on the effects of aerial bombing raids and civil provisions; but it was neither published nor acted upon. Of children made eligible for official evacuation, only 20 per cent left the city, possibly the lowest proportion in the country. Unlike in the metropolis, the civic authorities of Coventry had had no gradual introduction to the effects of *blitzkreig* devastation, nor the kind of provisions and services needed to repair a shattered infrastructure, or care for an all but shattered populace.

Coventry, like other cities, had taken some basic precautions, with blackout and air-raid shelters. The cathedral's great wide windows could not be covered, and so services were held at 3 p.m.; then, lamps were used with big protective shades. By summer 1940, sirens were sounding, and people sent running to the shelters. In these unpleasant, smelly places, the city's clergy and ministers held their services. But how to protect the cathedral? It was realized from the first that the building's physical form counted against its protection. A high-pitched roof, such as at Lincoln, would deflect incendiaries, or at least collect them in the parapet-gutter, where it would be easier to deal with them. On a nearly flat roof, they would simply burn where they landed. Painting KIRCHE (German for 'church') on the roof was suggested, in case the enemy might respect such things, but it was considered that they would not. The glass of the apse and clerestory windows was removed, over several months, and stored in the cellars of Hampton Lucy rectory. There was a plan to cover the roof with earth, which would render incendiaries less harmful, and aid their removal. It might have worked; but such a weight of material on such a roof might have caused the building to collapse: it was a gamble, and no earth was put in place. Buckets of sand and water were installed, along with stirrup-pumps and shovels. People were needed to operate these implements, and human resources were in short supply. With difficulty, four fire-watchers or guards were found to stand on the building at night; sometimes, though, no one was available, and Provost Howard and his wife were there alone. In the days before the bombing, Christians of all denominations worshipped together in St Michael's, praying for the leaders of the world, for those engaged in war, and for the enemy. These services caused Howard to conceive of a special place where these different kinds of Christians could perpetually worship together as one, a 'chapel of unity'. The war got grimmer, and London was time and again the target for attack. Then Coventry was attacked, and on the night of 14 October, an incendiary bomb landed on the cathedral roof, melted the lead, and started a fire. The fire was extinguished, but the damage, according to the report of cathedral architect Randoll Blacking, was valued at £1,180. Howard then made plans to move the best of the historic woodwork (e.g. the stalls with misericords) to a safer place; but time, and the affronted Nazi leader, would not allow it.

As the 'pathfinder' formation neared its target, Provost Howard, stonemason 'Jock' Forbes, and two young men, assembled on the roof, ignorant of what was in store for them. Soon after, at 7 p.m., the sirens went; five minutes later, the planes were there. Eight hundred and eighty-one incendiary canisters were released onto the centre of the town. Fires were seen all around St Michael's, and getting nearer and nearer. At about 7.45, the building was hit for the first time. One incendiary landed on the chancel roof, another crashed to the nave floor, and another landed on the south chancel aisle, above the organ. The alarm was given, and fire brigade requested, by shouting across to the nearby police station. The chancel bomb was covered with sand and thrown over the side, that in the nave was doused and shovelled up, but the one in the south chancel aisle had melted the lead and set the oak ceiling ablaze. Lead was hacked away, sand poured down the hole, and water pumped up from beneath; it was extinguished. The next devices landed on the Capper's Chapel, to the south, and the Smith's, to the north. The fire brigade had not arrived.

Meanwhile, at Holy Trinity, the vicar, Graham Clitheroe, had his fire-watchers on the roofs, their operations co-ordinated by a system of telephones that all connected with a nerve-centre manned by his sons in the north porch (Holy Trinity's roof-areas, and hence fire-watchers, would have been almost completely separated by the central tower); soon, Clitheroe's men were engaged in the same dangerous tasks as Howard's. At the cathedral, they managed to deal with the bombs on the outer-aisle roofs, but then, a great shower of canisters landed on the building, four seemingly above the Girdler's Chapel, and all four fire-fighters were at work again. Three holes in the roof were visible, with timber seen blazing inside, and smoke pouring out above. Sand and water were running out; the brigade had still not arrived. One of the fire-watchers tried to get to a tap situated in the Smith's Chapel, but smoke was thick there, and the man, half overcome, had to be helped back to safety. The fire could no longer be fought alone. The whole city was now ablaze. By this time, the planes with high explosive bombs had begun their work; it was probably such a device that hit Ford's Hospital, killing eleven inmates, and badly damaging the sixteenth-century timber structure. Howard and his exhausted men set about trying to carry and drag as much of the furnishings as possible, to safety, firstly from the Smith's Chapel, then from the vestries. Armfuls of silverware and vestments were carried across to the police station. Then, they could do little more than huddle in the south porch, try to keep warm, and wait for the fire engines. On the north side, the crypt chapels were serving as public shelters, where many others huddled, the building above them burning. Fire engines had been despatched from far and wide (one came from Wigan, Lancashire). To the vestry door, at 9.30, came the brigade from nearby Solihull. Hoses were set up all around the building, some dragged around by a sixteen-year-old fireman who lacked proper headgear; and water finally flowed onto the burning roof. The fire-watchers continued removing all that could be carried away, but had to watch idly as the Lady Chapel's screen and misericorded-stalls burned; and then the water ran out. The fire-watchers comforted the people in the crypt chapels, and another hydrant was found; but it had no water also. At 10.30 a hydrant was found which still had a supply, and a hose was trained on the Lady Chapel; but this water soon ran out as well. The city's water mains had been wrecked (presumably hit by high explosive bombs), and soon there was no water left at all. The firemen left the cathedral, never to re-enter it; an exhausted and dispirited group of people knew that the roof and all of the woodwork was lost. Howard then fancied he saw the effects of stone melting, under the intense heat of burning oak; but he felt sure that the walls of stone should still survive.

A short distance away stood one pile of stone whose life seems charmed, the octagonal tower and spire of the Grey-friar's church. Built c.1350, it survived the destruction of its church when the friary was dissolved in the sixteenth century, and in 1830–32 Christ Church was added to it by architects Rickman and Hutchinson. On this night, the church escaped destruction, but perished in the raids of 1941. In modern times, Coventry has been known as the 'city of three spires' (as in Tennyson's poem); the Greyfriar's spire (230 feet/70.10 metres) was the third. It survived the destruction of Christ Church, and still stands today. At Holy Trinity, though not engulfed by fire-bombs, some high-explosives landed very close, and Clitheroe records the horrific sensation of being upon, and in, a medieval church as it was felt to shake.

Around 11 p.m., Provost Howard carried the books of the Epistles and Gospels from the vestry to the police station; they were the last things to leave. From the police station's porch he and the others watched in horror as the whole interior began to collapse. Everyone had forgotten the iron, J. O. Scott's iron girders, hidden within timber beams in the 1880s, to tie the clerestory walls together. When structural metal is heated, it buckles and bends, and the structure often fails as a result. Modern structural steelwork is required to have effective protection against fire, but in the nineteenth century there were no codes of practice or methods of design for protection against fire; and this is generally considered the prime cause of the major structural collapse, the internal colonnades and clerestory. The outer walls were not affected by this factor. The people in the crypt heard the crashing of masonry above them, and were led away to a safer place. Howard had hoped that the vestries, around and below the apse, would at least be safe; but the fire spread there from the Mercer's Chapel, and one by one they, too, perished. When morning came, only the outer walls stood, the remnants of all else contained within them in a grim tangle of broken masonry and metal; but high above, the great tower stood, hard and strong.

The raid had lasted for about ten hours; involving 449 aircraft, it was perhaps the most intense single attack on any British city. 503 tons/511 tonnes of high explosive were dropped, almost twice the amount dropped on any London borough in the heavy onslaughts of the previous month. A third of homes were destroyed or rendered uninhabitable and useless, likewise over 400 shops, most railway lines, and other services and communications. The streets, mostly impassable, were piled high with rubble. 554 people were dead, some lying far below the ruins; 865 were seriously injured. Two hospitals had been hit. On the morning of Friday 15 November, a dazed and damaged people emerged to find their city thus destroyed, and its ancient cathedral destroyed with it. Accounts differ as to how they reacted and behaved in these almost unbelievable circumstances. Some members of the independent fact-gathering group Mass Observation arrived, and their reports tell of dazed and stupefied citizens, their faces covered with soot, wandering around aimlessly, knowing no purpose, direction, or hope. These accounts tell also of people screaming and fainting in the street, and of despairing men avowing that Coventry was finished and dead, its history over. Many were said to be seen leaving, some on foot, pushing prams and hand-carts, or fighting for vehicles. Other reports, however, stress the way people helped one another, the lack of panic, and the total absence of outbreaks of crime or irrational finding of scapegoats. Certainly, people were initially stunned, and the civic authorities were also reported to be shocked and useless, having had no preparations or experience. A cordon was thrown around the city, but a woman journalist managed to drive through it, and saw scenes of devastation unknown outside. This was Friday evening, and a depressing drizzle poured down. In such situations, people become confused and irrational. Stories, weird and groundless, began to spread, such as the claim that a German plane had landed on the roof of the Co-op, and that the cathedral tower had been left standing by the Germans on purpose, so that the bombers could use it to locate the city again, for they were sure to be back. But on Friday night, the bombers returned to London, and a mere eight planes got to Coventry.

There are many ironies involved in the destruction of Coventry and its cathedral—some have emerged in our story already—and among them is the fact that in purely military terms, it was an almost total failure. Twelve aircraft factories were hit, but though the buildings were damaged (600,000 feet/182,880 metres) of roof was removed from the Morris engine plant) the vital machines inside were either operable or repairable. Production was stopped for only *one* day, and after four further days production was back to full capacity, British aircraft manufacture exceeding that of Germany, in the overall 1940 figures. Had the bombers returned in force on the night of the 15th, the story would have been different, but they failed to; as it was, British troops began flooding into the city on that day, and many more came in the days that followed. The soldiers cleared rubble and restored services; an important part of their work was getting the factories working again. Some were detailed to demolish buildings rendered dangerous by the bombs. One such man, observing that the cathedral tower leant a little out of true, presumed structural damage, and prepared to blow it up. A passer-by, whose chance presence should be recorded in the annals of architectural conservation, asked the soldier what he was doing, and promptly told him that it had stood thus for centuries. The soldier desisted, the passer-by walked on, and the great tower continued its journey down the path of history, so very nearly halted (concern was later voiced nationally about the amount of probably unnecessary destruction of historic buildings, in precisely this way).

How long it took the German high command to discover the *military* failure of the raid is uncertain, but they immediately capitalized on the psychological value. Nazi propaganda devised the word *Coventrieren*, to *Coventrate* or incinerate a city at a blow, and, in an attempt to break morale, threatened to Coventrate the cities of Britain one by one.

The horrific events of November 1940 are crucial to our understanding of Coventry Cathedral as it came to be, and the powerful experiences, feelings, and beliefs that eventually shaped it, and to which, for many, it gave expression. In Provost Howard's account of his cathedral's burning (in his *Ruined and rebuilt* (1962)), it is clear that from the time of the

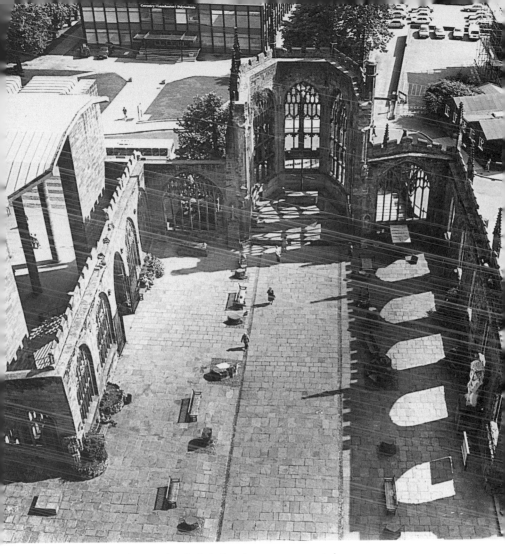

The ruined cathedral, from its tower, as seen today.

fire, events, of themselves, supplied a spiritual didacticism whereby the experience of event and accident was as a fabric in which happening and truth were woven into one. He suggests no conscious devising of the relation of this destruction with Jesus Christ's death, for instance, but rather he tells how the burning of the church ineluctably presented to him that original dying, and rebirth. It is obvious that in the events of the fire which he records, Howard and his helpers time and again risked their lives and faced their own deaths. A short while after the cathedral's destruction, a photograph appeared in the *Daily Mirror* which looks down from the tower onto the open bare walls, and the mounds of blackened rubble within. At the centre someone noticed the presence of a cross, itself broken and bent, composed of two fallen fragments of the unfortunate iron. To Howard and many others it seemed that in this burning, Christ suffered anew with his people, and that as he had risen from his perishing, so would they, their city and their cathedral. At 10 a.m. on the 15th, Howard was photographed by a local newspaper-man, standing beside the ruins affirming 'we shall build it again'. Though seeming to some to be isolated and alone in its destruction, Coventry quickly reached the headlines of the world's press, and for the visual image to convey this inhumanity and barbarism, the gutted cathedral seems automatically to have suggested itself. This church's destruction at the hands of human evil, its suffering and dying amongst its immolated people, became a symbol by no crude contrivance or image-making, nor from that subtle craft of imagination with which artists create icons of inert matter, but by some virtual process of its own.

Howard relates how to him the building's piles of broken masonry still seemed to contain some power transcending wholeness or design or the structured form imposed by human hand; and with time, this feeling of his increased. The possible part played by physical matter and objects in the human experience of the divine, and their role in worship and spirituality is a continual problematical fascination of those who study religious architecture and art. In 1958, Howard received a letter from a woman telling him of an experience she had had some while before, when visiting the cathedral ruins. From her account, the *place*, and the objects within it, were some part of the cause of an experience by which she says she found complete and lasting faith in Jesus Christ.

Attempts to define the nature and function of religious art will of necessity recur in any attempt to evaluate modern cathedrals and churches, and certainly such questions are important in this present study. The creation and potential of religious symbols is seen strongly in the story of the Coventry 'Cross of Nails'. The origin of this cross is hard to determine exactly, but it must surelty be linked with the many moving and meaningful experiences—such as the one related by

OPPOSITE: *Ruined St Michael's. This modern view shows a fragment of the clerestory, which ran east. The spire of Holy Trinity is seen beyond.*

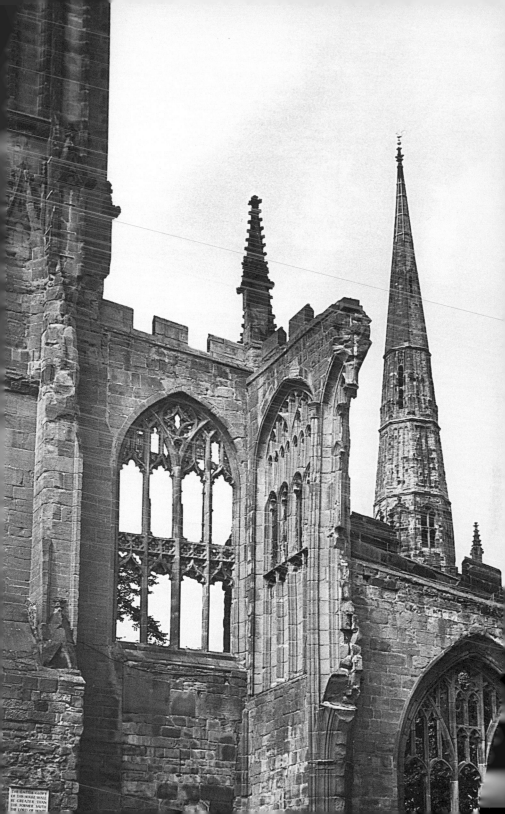

Howard's female correspondent of 1958—that people have had within the cathedral ruins. On the morning after the burning, a Coventry clergyman, Rev A. P. Wales, is said to have found three large nails which once joined the roof-beams together. He bound them together with wire, and showed the resulting cross to the bishop. Three months later, Provost Howard showed a student friend, Stephen Verney, around the ruins, and he likewise picked up some nails, and bound them together. Before long, Howard and others realized the power of symbolism contained within this poignant little construction, with its reference, via the original purpose of the nails, to the glorious building, destroyed so needlessly, and thence to the nails of Jesus's crucifixion. The cross of nails rapidly became not only a symbol of Coventry, but of destruction and sacrifice (with the implicit power of rebirth) in any place or time. Soon after its making, a cross of nails was being presented by the cathedral to people all over the world, in acts of friendship, reconciliation, and witness. Eventually, the Community of the Cross of Nails was established, with chapters in many countries.

In January 1941 Howard got Jock Forbes to build an altar, just forward of the site of the previous high altar. It was composed of pieces of broken masonry, with some suitable lengths of moulding as vertical corner-pieces. The altar's top or *mensa* was made of some slate tombstones. From among the ruins, two burnt beams were taken, and wire used to join them. This cross was set up in a tub of sand. Some time later, at the rear of this altar, the words *Father Forgive* were carved. In Holy Week of that year, there was another heavy raid. Incendiaries landed among the ruins, powerful high-explosives damaged St Mary's Hall, and Holy Trinity shook again. On Good Friday and Easter Day, services were held amidst the cathedral ruins.

When Coventry Cathedral was destroyed, some people grimly feared that it might be just the first of many. Mercifully, this was not so, and this is one reason why Coventry remains the supreme example of such destruction. We have seen that the raid was not aimed at churches or historic buildings, and thus it should never be confused with the so-called 'Baedeker' raids of 1942. These were staged in retaliation for the Allied attacks on the historic city of Cologne. The 'Baedeker' was a German cultural guide-book, and, from the volume for Britain, the Luftwaffe are supposed to have selected

The Charred Cross, made from burned beams, and the simple altar, made from fragments of stone, set up shortly after the cathedral's destruction.

targets from the historic towns. In these raids, Exeter Cathedral's chapel of St James was destroyed, and Canterbury Cathedral's library. Canterbury, like Coventry, removed historic glass, emptying its windows, and the nave was filled with earth up to about the height of a person; tombs were covered in sandbags. In London, St Paul's received two direct hits, and there were two very near misses; in the 1930s, surveyor Godfrey Allen had replaced Wren's internal stone rubble with liquid concrete, thus toughening the structure against high explosive shocks. Llandaff Cathedral—the only other to suffer damage comparable with that of Coventry—was reduced to ruins by a land-mine in 1941.

At Liverpool Cathedral we see how great churches could serve to locate targets: its roofs—vast, though half their eventual size—were covered in some material that reflected the dangerous moonlight. Any such fixed point could help the navigators locate the docks; when the dean and chapter became aware of the situation, the roofs were promptly given a special non-reflective coating. Many parish churches were destroyed in the war, of course, and the blitz was the occasion (though not, it is often argued, the cause) for the loss of yet more of Wren's city churches, the origin of which reminds us that medieval churches and cathedrals had perished in fire-storms long before the development of aerial bombing. In the First World War none of this 'cultural destruction' could have happened: the Kaiser threatened to hang any of his Zeppelin pilots whose bombs damaged Buckingham Palace, Westminster Abbey, or the Houses of Parliament; no such threats were made in the Second World War, of course, and the House of Commons was wrecked by a bomb in May 1941.

Soon after the cathedral's destruction, serious consideration was given to exactly what was to be done. Should a completely new church be built on the same site, should a new church be built on another site, or should the previous building simply be reconstructed? Other possibilities included the use of another existing church as cathedral, either Holy Trinity, or St Mary's, Warwick. And if the same site was *not* to be used, what should be done with the ruins? If a new building on the site was planned, what *then* should actually be done with the remains? Howard suggested to the Cathedral Council that they appoint, as their architect, Sir Giles Gilbert Scott (1880–1960), and this took place, in May 1942. Giles Scott was the nephew of John Oldrid, St Michael's restorer, and a grandson of Sir Gilbert.

Howard says that he admired Giles's great work, Liverpool's Anglican cathedral (built 1904–80), a church built in an original gothic style in hard pink stone. In an attempt to overcome their dilemma as to *what* to build (if anything), the Cathedral Council then asked for advice from the Central Council for the Care of Churches, who asked an advisory group to visit and make recommendations. This group included Lord Esher, architect Professor Albert Richardson, church architect Charles Nicholson, and a clutch of deans. They suggested, in what is sometimes called the 'Esher report', the building of a new cathedral, but with the retention of both the remaining outer walls and the tower's visual prominence (removing it was never considered or allowed). They recommended a building in a style not copied from the old, but of a 'cathedral-like character', and in keeping with the remains. This was in effect advice *against* a modern style. They advised against a competition for a design (after the Guildford Cathedral competition, Richardson wrote scathingly of the competition system, that its 'story will not bear analysis'). Meanwhile, Coventry's city architect Donald Gibson, advised the use of a modern style, as whatever was built would have to sit amongst the new city developments, designed in the new modern architecture of which Gibson was an advocate; these redevelopments were envisaged *before* the war, of course. The Cathedral Council accepted the advice of the Central Council's group, and Scott proceeded with his work.

Giles Scott had been commissioned to build Liverpool Cathedral after winning a competition held in 1902. This competition had caused a noisy controversy in the architectural world, because its conditions had stipulated use of a gothic style, a requirement deeply resented by many architects as a limiting of artistic freedom and as counter-productive of 'progress' in architecture—both notions dear to the Edwardians. At this time, there was a great move away from the Gothic Revival of the previous century towards the rediscovery of various classical styles, and the necessity of a gothic style even for churches was by many considered *passé* (for churches, this new classicism contributed to interest in, and use of, the Early Christian, Byzantine and Baroque styles). In this respect, the controversy was a revival of the 'Battle of the Styles' of Sir Gilbert's day (the Foreign Office (1856–62) and Law Courts (1866–74) debacles, issues of gothic *versus* classic). It also involved ideas about the nature of architecture and the role of the architect, which had been aired in the so-called 'architecture—profession or art?' debate of 1892. In addition, this 1902 event caused some serious thinking about the purpose and form of cathedrals such as had not taken place, say, when Truro had been commissioned (1878), and this discussion went on in church circles also, some clergy saying that a new cathedral in Liverpool was unnecessary. Fortunately for Scott, and Liverpool's many admirers, the building went ahead.

In 1932, Edward Maufe (1883–1974) won a competition to build a cathedral on another new, hill-top site, at Guildford (a diocese created from Winchester in 1927). Maufe was a church architect whose work was mostly in a very restrained gothic style, and often used brick, and Guildford is no exception to these. Unlike most other cathedral competitions, that for Guildford seems to have caused hardly a murmur of protest or controversy; perhaps the outcome at Liverpool—where the clause requiring gothic had been rescinded, without affecting the final result—had made architects become resigned to gothic Anglican cathedrals for the next few decades. Maufe's cathedral began construction in 1936, and while much work was done before the war, a major portion was built in the years 1952–61. In the 1930s, when Giles Scott was still building in gothic (among other styles) a new battle, long looming, came to a head, that between historical or traditional architecture, and that of the Modern Movement. The latter, which involved the idea of a total break with the past, originated on the Continent in the 1920s, and while its importation to Britain was slow, its coming was accelerated by the arrival of refugees from Europe, in the later 1930s. Scott, in his inaugural address as President of the Royal Institute of British Architects (in November 1933) saw this 'modernism *versus* traditionalism' as merely a new version of the old nineteenth-century 'Battle of the Styles'. Scott had a non-doctrinaire, non-ideological, attitude to architecture and styles—historical or modern—considering that artistic quality (a thing he saw as being independent of the style involved) was what mattered.

In December 1942, Scott received a letter from the headmaster of Blundell's School, Tiverton, Devon. He could only manage to reply that he would need time to adequately answer the many issues raised by his correspondent. This headmaster, Neville C. Gorton, said that he was set to become the new Bishop of Coventry (following the translation to Winchester of Mervyn G. Haigh, Coventry's third bishop (1931–42)).

Gorton's amazing mercurial mind showered Scott with schemes, ideas, hopes and visions (no wonder poor Scott had to pause for thought on getting the first drenching!); prominent among these was the desire for a free-standing altar at the new cathedral. Gorton said the idea was that of his friend the artist Eric Gill (1882–1940), with whom he had set up such an altar at Blundell's, and Gill had produced a free-standing altar in his church in Norfolk. St Peter, Gorleston on Sea (1938–39) did have a free-standing altar beneath suspended ciborium, and in his *Mass for the masses* (published in his *Sacred and secular* (1940)) Gill defended the idea of an altar brought forward, rescued from the 'mystery mongering of obscure sanctuaries separated from people'. However, Gill obviously did not invent or even revive the idea, since it had been used at the important churches of St Philip, Cosham, Portsmouth (1938, J. N. Comper), St Anslem, Kennington, London (1933, Adshead and Ramsey), St Mary, Wellingborough (1908–30, J. N. Comper), Westminster Cathedral (1895–1903, J. F. Bentley), Holy Redeemer, Clerkenwell, London (1887–88, J. D. Sedding), and many others. Its use was a conscious revival of Early Christian and Byzantine forms and arrangements, sometimes by way of Italian post-Tridentine Baroque, and it is from this latter source that Gill surely came by it, being a convert to Roman Catholicism. In seeing the centralized, forward altar as a means to make the liturgy more alive and intelligible to the ordinary worshipper, however, Gill was probably responding to other influences and ideas which we must examine below.

Gorton arranged to meet Scott, telling him that Provost Howard agreed with him about the altar (though a little earlier, Howard seems to have had reservations about a central altar because of its effects on preaching and the siting of pulpits). Scott was accommodating—with Gorton he probably *had* to be. He delved into his notebooks and found the church of Moulin-sur-Jeure, near Nevers, which had a double-altar beneath baldacchino, with bishop's seat set close by; and besides, in 1922–24 Scott had designed an altar beneath baldacchino for his chapel of Ampleforth Abbey, North Yorkshire. The other matter that they discussed was the facility for Christians of many denominations to use the cathedral together. Under Gorton—enthroned amidst the ruins on 20 February 1943—Howard's original idea of a chapel was supplemented with that of a Christian centre in which, and from which, service could be given to the community. The constitution of this centre or centres was published in 1944, and this formed another item in Scott's brief. In the church at large some were strongly opposed to the united facility, but Archbishop William Temple supported it, as we should guess, as later did Archbishop Fisher, and the legal moves against it in Convocation were in due course fought off. Gorton and Howard were not the only forward-looking clergymen with whom Scott was exploring new ideas in the first half of the 1940s: it was at this time that he and Liverpool's Dean Dwelly discussed the yet-to-be-built nave at Liverpool. The eventual product of their work was the concept of a nave which was a slightly separate space, in which other, less-formal, kinds of worship could take place, and other activities and events.

In February 1944 Scott unveiled his scheme. It met with all the requirements drawn up in 1942, and those of Bishop Gorton (in his account of his proposal, Scott refers to a 'United Christian Service Centre', administered by a joint council of Anglicans and Free-churchmen: but the chapel and the centre are separate, though linked). But already, Gorton's mind seems to have moved on. By November he was telling Scott of a noisy meeting at Coventry in which there was 'virulence, controversy and hate'. Everyone, he said, but particularly the clergy, wanted a *new* cathedral, a modern-style church; and probably, by this time, *he* did. Scott could do, would do, what was asked for; but formerly he had been instructed to produce a building in keeping with ruins and tower! So Scott re-cast the *interiors* in a modern style, a style that he had been developing in the later 1930s, having origins in his designs for the Forth Road Bridge, and other non-religious work. All records of the first interior have vanished, but the later interior employed great white surfaces, intersecting volumes, and pure unarticulated arches (parabolic, but with gothic points at the top). Within this was an altar topped with coronet-like baldacchino. An example of this kind of style is Scott's Carmelite church, Kensington (1954–59). Many liked this design when, drawn in perspective by A. C. Webb, it was released and exhibited at the Royal Academy (from May 1945). Above all, perhaps, the bishop liked it. The arrangement of both schemes was a large rectangular volume, set north–south, towards the eastern end of St Michael's. The altar was placed half-way along this, and

OPPOSITE: Giles Gilbert Scott's scheme for a new cathedral, perspective of interior of principal volume. Interior as developed 1944—5, in response to Bishop Gorton's ideas.

the old apse projected through the volume, to the east. The remaining ancient outer-walls, to the west, were used to make cloisters, with an area equipped with a pulpit, for outside services, within the garth. A Chapel of Unity and a Lady Chapel (rectangles) projected east from the main volume, connecting with a very long range (the Christian Service Centre), enclosing another quadrangle within, the Centre parallel to the main church.

In July 1946 Gorton and Howard asked the Royal Fine Art Commission (RFAC) to evaluate Scott's design. They appeared before the commission on the 12th of the month, and suggested that while the Cathedral Council and Diocesan Conference had accepted it, there were still some 'unsatisfactory features relating to the proposals' and plans could 'still only be regarded as provisional'; these words seem to contain the suggestion of a prompt, and following a visit by the commissioners, in November, they reported that they were unable to approve the design, and recommended that it be abandoned. Their objection may well have been to the use of different styles for the inside and outside of the building. Many people were opposed to any reconstruction of historic buildings in a similar style or sympathetic manner (an idea that may have its origins in the sanctimonious attitude to medieval architecture found in some of the less-sagacious writings of William Morris); these ideas may have been held by some of the RFAC members. In the last years of the war, Scott had been commissioned to restore the House of Commons; naturally, Scott's House would be 'in keeping' which was deplored by some.

Scott sent his resignation to Coventry, and his letter stressed his age (66) and inability to direct construction of the eventual design, whatever it was (for this reason, he had only been commissioned for an initial five years); and then the old questions, choices, and problems returned.

Chapter Five

1947 TO 1962

CONTROVERSY AND COMPETITION

ON 8 JANUARY 1947, six days after Scott's letter to them, the Cathedral Council met and accepted his resignation, and appointed the Harlech Commission. Following a statement by the bishop on 10 January, the actual members of the commission and their terms of reference were published in the architectural press. Clearly, the commission had been formed *before* Scott's letter of resignation (and in the previous month, December 1946, according to *The Builder* of 11 July 1947, presumably following the RFAC Chairman's letter to Bishop Gorton of 19 December). Lord Harlech's commission included the Provost of Leicester, the Bishop of Stafford, Sir Philip Morris (vice-chancellor of Bristol University) and the Rev E. Benson Perkins. Perkins, of the Methodist Church's Department of Chapel Affairs, had recently published (with Albert Hearn) *The Methodist Church builds again* (1946), an influential church-building manual of great practicality. After 10 January, Sir Percy Thomas (who had twice been President of the RIBA), was added.

The commission was appointed to hear evidence and advise on provision of a cathedral church, 'ancilliary buildings', and the cathedral's Christian Service Centre and Chapel of Unity. It met many times in the first half of the year, and considered the various possibilities, most of which had been investigated before: should a new site be used? Should the cathedral go elsewhere? Should Holy Trinity be used? Holy Trinity, still under Graham Clitheroe, considered that to build a new church was wasteful, in view of the proximity of theirs; but the commission considered it too small, with one half to two-thirds of seats not having sight of the pulpit. Could it be extended? An octagon, with central altar, could be added at the east (the idea of J. N. Comper), or, a new nave could be built to the north, with an altar beside the crossing and south transept; but it was understood that the RFAC would oppose such a scheme. St Mary's, Warwick, was again canvassed. Some Coventry architects argued that a new cathedral did not require the removal of the ruins. Once again, some favoured reproduction or reconstruction; former cathedral architect Randoll Blacking now advised that the walls would no longer support a roof, etc., as they had weakened considerably in the years since the destruction.

The commission reported on 10 July. They recommended a new cathedral on or near the site of the predecessor (but reported the insufficient strength of the existing walls to support a new structure). Originally considering a building seating 2,000, they now recommended one seating 1,000. A building in red sandstone was advised, designed inside and out in the English gothic tradition; it should not be a copy, but one avoiding violent contrast with that around it. An open competition for a design was suggested, to be organized by the RIBA, and the setting up of a Building Committee. They favoured inclusion of a choir in the church, and choir aisles seating 200 clergy (but no transepts) and an altar at the east end, in the traditional manner (but no screen). They favoured a rich, splendid interior for the church, with stone vaults if possible. Their report was traditionalist in tone throughout, to the surprise of many. When reporting its appointment on 17 January, *The Builder* had suggested that the commission 'will now recommend another architect, who will presumably design a building modern in its treatment throughout' (unlike Scott's); how wrong they were! The RIBA opposed the gothic clause, in their letter to the Cathedral Council of 16 July, as did the Coventry Society of Architects and City Architect Donald Gibson. On 19 July, a diocesan conference at Warwick accepted the report except for the reference to gothic. By August the Cathedral Council had changed the words 'in the English gothic tradition' to 'the architect being left free to make his own choice of style, provided that the new cathedral is built in continuity and harmony with the tower and spire' (the commission's recommended use of red sandstone remained). By this move, a repetition of the Liverpool Cathedral controversy, was averted, and, it seems, the modern-style cathedral that Gorton really wanted, had been brought one step nearer. However, no one seems to have made the slightest protest against the east end altar: Provost Howard records this recommendation, but makes no comment on it, nor do we learn of any objections from the bishop. Perhaps if his desire for a modern-style church *had* steadily increased, his wish for a central altar, may, by some curious inverse process, have decreased (in May 1947 Roger Pinckney and Arthur Gott had won the Colombo Cathedral competition (assessor: Giles Scott) with a design which included a forward-standing altar with baldacchino).

In wanting a modern building, but still accepting a clause requiring harmony with the old (and in red sandstone) the Cathedral Council were surely preparing another impossible situation for the next architect, just as— *The Builder's* leader-writer acknowledged—they had for Scott; or perhaps the bishop and Cathedral Council did not really understand what the new modern architecture really was. Had they or their advisers had a complete understanding of what was wanted and appropriate, they could more easily have proceeded by selecting a group of architects, known to be suitable, and inviting them to produce competition schemes (as had happened at St Mary's Episcopalian Cathedral, Edinburgh, in 1872), or by allowing the invited architects to compete by submitting past work, the person selected developing a cathedral design with the clients, after appointment (as had happened at Truro in 1878); but both procedures frustrate unknown young architects and new ideas.

Though in 1947, things seemed to be happening quickly, in the next two years there were no important developments. The need was felt to provide a site with greater possibilities for an architect, and the first steps were taken in the buying of land to the north of St Michael's. These negotiations were not without problems, including the difficult acquisition of a wine-merchant's cellars, which came complete with the unquiet spirit of a former monk; this work went on into the 1950s. In the spring of 1948, the cathedral was cleared of the ruined remains of the arcade, clerestory and roofs, and began to be re-planned and made more easily useable. Various arrangements have been effected there since 1940, but the first work involved

89

The cathedral in April 1948, looking west. The remains of the colonnades and clerestory were removed shortly afterwards, the central 'aisle' was made some years before (Bishop Gorton was consecrated in this setting in 1943).

the covering of the former church pavement with earth and grass, and the re-glazing of the tower. In the years since 1940, worship had gone on, and while the cathedral congregation had used Holy Trinity part of the time, use of the crypt chapels, the Chapel of the Resurrection (made out of the southern porch in 1942, (now the Haigh Chapel)) and the ruins themselves, produced a tradition of worship that had a great formative effect on that of the later years. On VE Day (8 May 1945) people flocked into the ruins, and all day and night acts of worship, thanksgiving and commemoration took place, in largely spontaneous expressions of relief mixed with loss. In 1944 and 1945 the ruins were used for staging religious drama, something which Coventry Cathedral was to become very well known for in later years, and these presentations formed a link with Coventry's religious past. As early as Christmas 1946, services of Christian unity and reconciliation with former enemies were being held in this place that had become filled with meaning, for so many. A product of the liturgical use of the ruins, in the early 1940s, was the eight 'Hallowing Places'. These were not altars or shrines, but wooden boards carved with inscriptions. The texts were prayers which referred to aspects of daily life, to the home and the work-place, to recreation and arts, commerce and education.

At the end of 1949, the Reconstruction Committee, created following Harlech's recommendations, began to make plans for the competition (its chairman, E. H. Ford, had been City Engineer). In January 1950, discussions were held with the RIBA under its president, Michael Waterhouse. In March, the RIBA nominated assessors who were appointed in May. They were Howard Robertson, Percy Thomas and Edward Maufe. Robertson was both a prolific architect and active in architectural education. Author of the influential *Principles of architectural composition* (1925) his most conspicuous work today, perhaps, is the Shell Centre on London's South Bank (1961–67). Thomas was a gifted Welsh architect whose origins were in the Edwardian Baroque of Cathays Park, Cardiff, but produced his best works in a severe cubic classicism, e.g. the Swansea civic centre (mid-1930s) and Cardiff's 'Temple of Peace' (1938). Maufe, the only church architect, and the only non-classicist, was a traditionalist, as seen in his cathedral at Guildford; yet his inter-war domestic work reflected Swedish modernism, and his *Modern church architecture* (1948) was devoted to the latest Continental church-building, illustrating the work of Schwartz, Bartning, Böhm, Perret, Moser and Sonck. The RIBA that selected these men was on the brink of a power-struggle, whereby the leaders of the older generation were replaced by the new men of Modernism. After meetings between the assessors and the bishop and provost, the competition was launched, and in the autumn the cathedral produced a brochure containing the conditions, a site plan, photographs of the ruins, etc., which was available till 22 December.

The conditions and requirements were many. They asked for: a church to seat 1,250, with stalls for 24 cathedral clergy and permanent seating for 150 diocesan clergy. The altar was to be at the liturgical east, but there was to be no screen. There must be room for 'liturgical movement'. Chapels to be incorporated included a Children's Chapel (seating 30), a Chapel of the Resurrection (seating 30), a Guild Chapel (seating 50), a Chapel of Unity ('contiguous with the main Cathedral building'), and a Lady Chapel (seating 75). The Christian Service Centre (to 'form an architectural composition with the Cathedral') was to have a meeting room, kitchen, reading room, Warden's flat, etc. Portions of the ruins to be retained included the tower and spire, the south porch, the crypts, and the Capper's Room (this last item would require restoration, however). Retention, or otherwise, of the other parts of the ruins was optional (and this included the apse). The buildings could be placed anywhere on the site, east–west orientation not being required. As to style, the conditions stated 'No restrictions are placed on competitors as to style', and while it was pointed out that nearby buildings, and the ruins, were in pink sandstone, and that similar stone was still available, there was *no* actual reference to the buildings needing to be 'in keeping'—or otherwise. The new cathedral was required to have specific situations for the Cross of Nails, the Charred Cross, the Altar of Rubble, and the Hallowing Places; the last of these could be re-created in a new medium, as desired. The Chapel of Unity was explained, the theological description connecting the chapel with Pentecost and the Holy Spirit. A statement on the nature of worship, for which it was to be designed, was added; it was to be a liturgy centred on the eucharist, and the altar—though not physically central—was to be visually pre-eminent, the church to be designed *around* the altar, rather than it being an altar placed in a church. It was referred to as the 'people's altar'.

The competition (restricted to qualified architects from

Britain, Eire and the Commonwealth) required entries to be submitted to the solicitor's office in Bayley Lane, from which it was organized, by 2 July 1951 (this was later changed to 20 July). Arrangements were made with the King Henry VIII School for the entries to be displayed and adjudicated there, and 567 copies of the conditions were sent out, plus a further document produced from answers given to the many questions received after the initial competition announcement. Architects were instructed to design works to the cost of £825,000 (estimated in October 1950), and war damage compensation was then assessed at about £604,000.

The publication of the competition conditions, combined with the recently revealed work at the reconstructed House of Commons, became the cause of an occasionally bitter controversy, begun in the columns of *The Times*, concerned with the appropriate form of additions— or whatever—to partially-destroyed historic buildings, and, arising from this, the whole nature, basis, and direction, of architecture itself. Robert Lutyens wrote a letter which argued that use of gothic should be prohibited in the competition conditions, and that the new House of Commons was a 'fake'. Replying to this, Scott repeated his belief that style was irrelevent to artistic quality, and that the historical styles, which were the product of long evolution, were able to express such profound things as religious faith because their 'language' had developed gradually over long centuries; the modern style, however, was so new that as yet it was incapable of expressing anything. Classicist Raymond Erith asked if Lutyens considered that 'contemporary' design was to be preferred because it was style-less (and Lutyens seemed to be against styles), or because he considered it to be a superior style. Laurence Whistler wrote to the effect that good architecture was *not* produced by harmony with the past, and that great works often displayed the opposite of the 'neighbourly good manners' which Curtis Green had called for, at Coventry. In January 1951, Nikolaus Pevsner wrote an article in the *Architectural Review* which criticized these various positions from the point of view of a staunch defender of the Modern Movement. He argued that the great architectural styles had come into existence suddenly, by revolution, not evolution, and that the Modern Movement architecture was of this kind; it had been produced by the 'spirit of the age' which in each epoch creates the one authentic form of architecture. Pevsner preferred this kind of architecture, which, expressive or not, was 'at least alive', and, whatever its effect, was 'direct and whole'. Replying, E. Duck-Cohen pointed out that this spirit-of-the-age approach ultimately evaluated architectural works on the basis of the moment in time when they had been created, so that a gothic church was beautiful and valid if created in the fifteenth century, but unreal and bad if produced in the twentieth; to future generations, it will be the work itself, not the historical context of its creation, which will matter.

The first entry arrived on 25 May, and on 19 July folios were being delivered in great numbers. On the following, final, day, taxis laden with architects' submissions formed a traffic-jam along the approach to Bayley Lane. Each submission was numbered, the drawings hung in every part of the school buildings, and the names of their authors separated and locked in a safe. On 30 July, the assessors arrived.

On the second day of the adjudication, the architect of Guildford Cathedral collapsed into a chair and ordered a stiff drink. There had been 219 entries, and 1,491 drawings to be examined and evaluated. It was a long and difficult job, and the standard of most submissions, the assessors later claimed, was disappointing. But there were certainly some very novel and different designs. Rodney Thomas (Arcon) produced a great flowing roof ('sinoidal' in shape) which was set between the tower and apse: its form and appearance would have fitted perfectly with the new buildings of Brasilia; F. G. Lees's intersecting parabolic shells would likewise have blended with, say, the work of Affonso Reidy in Rio de Janeiro. David Aberdeen planned a large concrete octagon, to be sited north of St Michael's chancel, to be lighted by louvres on the south, east, and west sides. The scheme by local architect Rolf Hellberg had an interesting plan which included walls set at diagonals, with chapels in the resulting exedrae. It received a 'special mention' by the assessors, but was disqualified because of a failure to meet the requirements fully (allegedly, not allowing 'liturgical movement'). Perhaps the most successful modern-style entry was that of Alison and Peter Smithson, members of the younger generation of architects. This employed a shallow hyperbolic paraboloid, square in plan, which rose up from beside the tower to a point, supported on V-shaped struts. The scale of this simple form would have perfectly balanced the tower (through the base of which, the building was to be approached). Raymond Erith's chaste

Model of 1951 competition entry by Alison and Peter Smithson. View from north-east.

classical design had a free-standing altar beneath ciborium, with the Chapel of Unity (externally projecting) related to it. The design of Albert Richardson with E. A. Houfe and S. Holland, which was 'specially mentioned', was a gothic cathedral, which used the surviving apse to create a lovely free-standing octagonal Lady Chapel. Like many twentieth-century church-builders, Richardson and his team were inspired by the great fortress-like cathedral of Albi, in France.

DESIGN AND DEVELOPMENT

When the assessors finished their work, they awarded the first place and prize of £2,000 to design No. 9, which proved to be the work of Mr Basil Spence of 40 Moray Place, Edinburgh. Basil Urwin Spence was born on 13 August 1907 in Bombay, India; his parents were from Scotland. He was educated at George Watson's College, Edinburgh, the school of architecture of Heriot-Watt University, Edinburgh, then at the Bartlett school of architecture, at University College, London. After the Bartlett, he worked as an assistant at the office of Sir Edwin Lutyens, and then in the office of Rowand Anderson. In Edinburgh, he formed successive partnerships in the second half of the 1930s. The Bartlett's classical tradition, and the influence of Lutyens, were clearly formative for the young Spence. His time with Lutyens included work on some of the New Delhi buildings, and from their designer Spence is said to have acquired a capacity for monumentalism, drama and display—so vital an ingredient at New Delhi, of course—which was with him for the whole of his career. But while in this same office he is known to have read the writings of Le Corbusier, one of the founders and chief propagandists of the Modern Movement. Spence's conversion to the new architecture has been described as both partial and late in his development, the doctrines of Functionalism, and their strict application, never outweighing his natural romanticism and tendency to the dramatic. His early works embody these polarities: 'Griblock' (with Perry Duncan (1937–39)) was a large house in the 'International Modern' style, but also at this time he produced a house for a friend, in the Scots Baronial style. After the war, he gravitated to exhibition design, work in which he excelled. He was chief architect to three important exhibitions before the 1951 Festival of Britain, for which he designed the 'Sea and Ships' pavilion and was chief architect to the Heavy Industries exhibition. By the beginning of the 1950s, Spence began to feel that this kind of work had imprisoned him, like a type-cast actor. He decided to go to America, but just before he did this, he heard of the competition to build a replacement for Coventry's burnt-out cathedral. The day after the Coventry raid, as Staff Captain (Intelligence), Spence had reported the church's destruction to his General. Shortly after D Day, appalled by the unnecessary military destruction of beautiful churches that he had witnessed in Normandy, Spence dreamed of some day creating a cathedral of his own.

We know of these facts, and so many more, from Spence's own book, *Phoenix at Coventry. The building of a cathedral* (1962). Here, unlike in almost every other case, we have detailed information as to the ideas, beliefs, theories, and conceptions which created a great church, the architect's understanding of the work, and his intention in producing it. Spence tells us things that no architectural historian, relying on note-books and sketches, could ever discover, and the contrast of this

Sir Basil Urwin Spence, OM, PPRIBA, (1907–1976).

97

situation with that of earlier cathedrals and their builders—as readers of the earlier chapters of this book will immediately realize—could not be greater. In *Phoenix*, Spence describes what he acknowledges as his first *architectural* experience. It was not experience of a *building*, but of caves, spaces in natural rock in India, where a temple had been created by carving the material of the earth itself. There he experienced 'awe', 'timelessness' and 'mystery', sensations which we must surely understand in terms of the late-eighteenth century theory of the Sublime. It seems to me that enclosure within dark caves provides some kind of experience of the primordial essence of space itself; and after this came Spence's second architectural experience, that of the interior of York Minster—a human *re-creation* of the natural archetype he experienced in India (this latter event was in 1927 when he was a second-year architectural student). The associations of 'ancient rites' at Lascaux, Delphi and Zimbabwe also strongly affected him. When on a dull day in October 1950 Spence and his wife entered the ruins of Coventry Cathedral, Spence was, by his own account, 'deeply moved', feeling it to be a 'Holy Place', experiencing a 'feeling of reverence'. (This experience of, and understanding of, the holy, suggests that concept normally known as the *numinous*, as explicated in Rudolf Otto's *Das Heilige* (1917), sacrality characterized by sensations of awe, wonder, and fear, the supra-rational element, as Otto called it, of religion.) To Spence, the ruin was 'still a cathedral', having the skies as its roof. He then tells us that he saw the old cathedral as 'standing clearly for the Sacrifice, one side of the Christian Faith', and, 'I knew my task was to design a new one which should stand for the Triumph of the Resurrection'. Then, looking to the north of the old chancel, across St Michael's Avenue, to ground reserved for the new building, Spence 'got one of those pictures that architects sometimes get. This one, however, was unusually clear—a great nave and an altar that was an invitation to Communion, and a huge picture behind it. . . . I could not see the altar clearly but through the bodies of the Saints.'

On more than one occasion, Spence claimed that this vision, seen in his first few minutes at Coventry, provided the sole inspiration and source of his cathedral, which he then designed and developed without any radical re-thinking or basic change. The eventual building was thus the result of a process that we must consider intuitive, non-rational, and spontaneous. As we look at the production and development of the

actual scheme, we must observe how these initial processes
were reinforced and supplemented by others, and subjected to
the many factors that influence the making of a church. The
idea of a building to 'stand' for the Sacrifice and 'the Triumph
of the Resurrection' is perhaps the most crucial in the creation
of Coventry Cathedral. We saw that the association of the
cathedral's burning with crucifixion and Sacrifice, was made
long before the competition conditions and the Harlech Report; however, though seeing the destruction in this way, and
vowing that the building would 'rise again', Provost Howard
nowhere suggests, at least in his writings, that a post-war
building or complex of buildings, new, old, or both, should be
specifically designed to embody these religious doctrines. It
seems clear that Giles Scott was never briefed in terms that
included such ideas. When Scott was designing (1943–45), the
approach was dominated by the central altar, and then mod-
ernity (i.e. Bishop Gorton's influence. Though no one speech
can represent a man's attitudes, on one occasion, in April 1951,
Gorton claimed that the ruins should not be allowed to
represent Christianity in Coventry—he was here opposing the
ruins' retention—and criticized the 'false sentimental affection'
that they were acquiring.) However, by the time of the
competition conditions, ideas about the representation of
sacrifice and resurgence, in the future church, had possibly
surfaced among the ecclesiastics, because of the demand they
included, that the Cross of Nails, the Charred Cross, and the
Altar of Rubble be incorporated in the future building. This
requirement does not appear as the cause of Spence's initial
vision of the new and old joined together as a great religious
symbol—as it became. Certainly Spence, following this requirement, placed these items in the new church in his
competition design, but he tells us that it was Howard's
suggestion that they instead remain *in situ*, to which he readily
agreed (except the Cross of Nails, which formed part of the
main altar cross). However, in Spence's report, as part of his
entry—which we must refer to later—he refers only to the
'beautiful ruin' which should be preserved as a 'garden of rest',
and currently acts as an 'eloquent memorial to the courage of
the people of Coventry'.

A few hours after his first visit to the site, Spence produced a
sketch plan of his idea. It has a rectangular volume set on a north–
south axis, almost at right-angles to St Michael's chancel,
with which it connects (the building is thus *not* traditionally

99

oriented). On the eastern side, at its northern extremity, a small circular volume projects (this was to be his Guild Chapel), and on the western side a star-shaped volume projects at the southern extremity (this was to be his Chapel of Unity). Internally, the rectangle is subdivided laterally by two rows of columns. The altar was at north rather than the traditional, liturgical, east. This plan looks very similar to the final one. Back in Edinburgh, Spence worked on his design, often drawing late into the night, sustained only by J. S. Bach, after a day at the office (he was currently working on the Festival of Britain projects). His design then acquired a very important feature, the origin of which was often to be referred to in popular interviews. Having been prepared for a dental extraction—albeit only by local anaesthetic—Spence became unconscious, and dreamt of walking through his cathedral. The altar, he says, 'looked tremendous' and was 'backed by a huge tapestry'. Although conscious of beautiful light, he could see no windows. When he had proceeded some distance up the nave, however, he turned and looked back, and saw that the windows were zigzagged or saw-toothed. Spence acknowledges that this release of subliminal experience might simply have been the remembrance of a technique of architectural lighting that was known of. It seems, from his words, that this dream was the origin of the use of tapestry for the 'great picture'. His cheeky dentist wanted to bill him for the ideas he had received.

Bored with the frame-covered-in-glass architecture of his exhibition designs, Spence determined to produce a work that was solid, and employed stone walls. Significantly, while avoiding any gothic vocabulary, he decided to eschew the *avant garde* approach of his recent work, and attempt to provide a cathedral possessing continuity with the past, a sense of permanence, unity, and also vitality. For this reason, he planned to include some kind of vault (and the columns), and stained glass. Herein lies the source of the architectural (but not liturgical) compromise or contradiction or synthesis—depending on your point of view—that was to be, and perhaps always will be, the source of so much comment and critical reaction. Spence tells us that his architectural design was created (in pursuit of continuity with the older cathedral) by using a combination of two spatial rhythms derived from St Michael's internal columns and its window mullions (much later, for his Embassy Chancery, Rome (completed 1971) Spence was simi-

The cathedral's eastern wall, showing the side windows.

larly to employ two rhythms from the Mannerist architecture of Michelangelo's nearby Porta Pia). When the competition entry was complete, it became one of the many that were handed in on the very last day.

In a lengthy architect's report, Spence explained his design. The altar (of rubble) was the heart, and visual climax, of the new building, which would be linked to the old one by a glass screen wall on the south side, which could be lowered into the floor as required, and a porch (rising over St Michael's Avenue, a public right of way). The baptistery would be placed within the main volume on the western wall, opposite the Chapel of Unity, which is now written of as like a crusader's tent, as well as like a star. The Chapel of Unity was placed away from sight

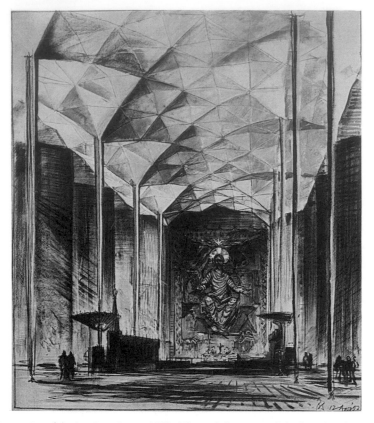

Perspective of the interior, August 1952. The vault has acquired the faceted or fly's eye effect; the tapestry, here, is set directly behind the high altar.

of the altar because an altar was not a requirement of the worship of Free Churchmen (for whom the Chapel was intended), but within sight of the baptistery, which was meaningful and acceptable to all Christians; Spence probably inserted these words because of his fear that lack of sight-line between the Chapel and main altar would go against him. In *Phoenix* he says that the conditions 'made clear' that such a view would be 'an advantage' to a competitor: in fact, the condition Clause 40, and the competition *Replies to questions*, 173–8, is highly confused and confusing. Some had visually linked the two (e.g. Raymond Erith). In terms of religious beliefs and 'proprieties', Spence here displayed a considerable grasp of the matter of Christian unity, and its implications for design. The structural system of the building was outlined: it

The 1953 model, which featured this vault (having a pierced faceted web, of concrete); note the reredos of lance-like verticals, which rises behind the high altar

involved a reinforced concrete shell roof raised on solid stone loadbearing walls, with concrete (reinforced or pre-stressed) internal columns, patterned stone floor, and concrete foundations. The assessor's report considered that the winning design 'shows that the Author has qualities of spirit and imagination of the highest order. He lets the Conditions grow under his hand to produce a splendid Cathedral . . .'.

When Spence heard of his premiation, he almost fainted. The winner of a major competition for such a building generally has the experiences of a struggling actor thrust instantly to stardom. His life was never to be the same again. Soon there were press conferences, interviews, articles—and abuse. Much of the criticism Spence suffered was mindless, twisted, or simply based on misunderstanding (no perspectives had been allowed in the competition, so the initial newspaper reproductions of his scheme were architectural projections and drawings of technical details, which often look aggressive to the untrained eye). Much of this reaction was not criticism or controversy of the kind we have examined above, and so is not relevant here, but there were exceptions. One is the article by J. M. Richards in the *Architectural Review* of January 1952. Richards, a propagandist of modern architecture, was quick to expose the various instances of old and new in the design [one cause of the general criticism was the design's ability to please neither 'traditionalist' nor 'modern' camp]. Not only was the scheme traditional in form—as a church—but *spatially* traditional (in its use of axes, as opposed to the new three-dimensional spatial subtleties allowed by modern building techniques). Spence's 'theatrical' architecture, Richards claimed, had produced a cathedral scheme filled with structural and physical contradictions. Not all informed opinion was negative in its assessment, however, for Nikolaus Pevsner supported the design, in a radio talk. But the criticism *did* play on Spence's natural sensitivities—even in a profession given to this trait, Spence seems to have stood out. Those who were not condemning the plan as old-fashioned were, like a clergyman in the Coventry diocese, likening it to a factory or 'mammoth insurance office'.

Few competition-winning architectural designs are built exactly as first entered, and while Spence's had no radical change, it was subjected to considerable development (Guildford's competition design, exceptionally, looks identical to the final product; at Liverpool, Scott totally re-shaped his building after about six years on site!). Spence's 'vision', his basic plan and volumes, did indeed remain unchanged; but the actual effect of a building on users and visitors often owes much to such things as surface treatments and finishes, lighting, furnishing, and artworks, and these Spence did change—at times radically—and essentially for the better. The developments were gradual and often localized, and can be charted from successive plans, elevations, perspectives, and models. Many architects would, reasonably, bury the earlier ideas, their less-certain steps on the road to perfection; but Spence openly and courageously made a large amount of such material widely available in *Phoenix at Coventry*. The documents include (chronologically): (1) the first (1950) sketch plan; (2) the 1951 competition drawings (which were widely published in the

The nave's vault, or vault-like canopy, seen from directly below. The multi-faceted web is made up of thousands of Sitka spruce slats.

architectural press, of course, e.g. *Architects Journal*, 23 August 1951); (3) Laurence Wright's exterior perspective (August 1951); (4) interior perspective, September 1951; (5) interior perspective, November 1951; (6) exterior perspective, July 1952; (7) interior perspective, August 1952 (p. 102); (8) interior perspective, February 1953; (9) model, 1953; (10) interior perspective, March 1958 (p. 103); (11) model, 1961.

The developments are perhaps best noted thematically. We saw that the characteristic zig-zag walls were absent in (1), but present in (2). The first porch (2) rose only half the height of the southern façade, and on the drawings looks small and feeble; the blank featureless wall above—suggestive, as we might expect, of Festival of Britain architecture—would have been visually less than pleasant, and suggest a municipal swimming bath. In January 1952 the Reconstruction Committee were asked to approve the far superior new porch, seen in an oblique perspective reproduced with J. M. Richards' article of this same month, and (6). In this scheme, the porch's canopy is set at full height, and the blank wall mercifully gone. In (6), *roods* are inserted high up between the slender columns (i.e. the crucified Christ with figures of Mary and St John). Later, these became plain wooden crosses. This new porch created the great southern window, or screen wall, of course (it is often referred to as the 'west' window, i.e. liturgical west). The lowering, opening, window had been condemned by Spence as a gimmick.

At first, Spence intended the Hallowing Places to be set on the blank portions of the zig-zag walls, with large sculptures above, in the manner of side-chapels (4). Bishop Gorton objected to additional altars and suchlike, presumably because they were competing secondary foci. Eventually, the sculptures and Hallowing Places went; the latter, eventually re-carved in slate, remained *in situ* in the ruins, the original wooden ones being re-sited behind No. 11 Priory Row. The 1953 model (9) (p. 103) shows the blank wall with lower, rectangular sculptures, which are well on the way to their final form: the Tablets of the Word ((10), March 1958).

In his competition entry report, Spence refers to the stone walls that are to be visible inside and out. By March 1958, it has been decided that inside they will be covered with white rendering, which made a considerable difference from pink sandstone. Before the 1953 model (9), a tapestry-representation by Spence had been included in drawings, but this and later documents include current stages in the development of Graham Sutherland's design. In the competition entry, Spence indicated a strange steel object to rise above the font. He likened it to a fir-cone; it looks on perspectives more like the chimney to some tasteless Scandinavian free-standing fireplace, or some phallic pagan megalith. In the final design there was no font cover at all.

The changes to the vault contribute a significant modification to the scheme, and it is a feature that has considerable effect on the 'feel' of the building. At first, the vault was to have been one composed of flowing curves, very similar indeed to groin vaults, particularly if compared with the stuccoed, white, Italian version (this vault required *four* rows of columns). In August 1952 (7) the faceted or fly's eye effect is present (p. 102). In the 1953 model, the vaulting panels have been perforated with triangular holes, making the whole into a kind of mesh (p. 103). The use of slatted spruce produces the effect we have today, the basic form of the vaulting panels being visible in the March 1958 perspective.

Much attention has been given above to the nature and position of the altar. Though the competition conditions suggested a traditional altar at the liturgical east, and Spence designed one in his entry, in post-competition discussions with the cathedral authorities, Gorton again pressed for a forward, open-sided altar, an idea supported by his friend Fr C. E. Douglas. In November 1951, Spence produced a scheme with the altar forward, within a U-shape space created by the choir seated at the side, and clergy behind, with the bishop centrally behind the altar, in a version of the ancient basilican arrangement, as in the churches of Ravenna which Spence admired. This setting no longer fitted Spence's original sequence of colours in the side-windows, and the desired colour of light thrown on the altar, but he agreed to it. Then, however, he tells us of a meeting of the Reconstruction Committee in which a 'near riot' broke out over the new position of the altar, and they reverted to the old position. Spence gives no date for this meeting, and the Committee's papers in the cathedral archives, seem to be silent about this matter; and strange it is that a man possessed of the determination and charisma of Gorton could not win a committee over to his side. In his chapter on Gorton, in F. Moyle's book, Spence tells us that the bishop accepted the decision, and backed the architect's original arrangement.

At first, the Lady Chapel was to have been *behind* the great tapestry. By February 1953, the 'tapestry wall' has reached the far north (i.e. liturgical east) of the building, and the high altar is backed by a reredos of lance-like vertical members ((9), and (10), March 1958). Eventually, (11) the reredos disappeared entirely, but a grille of similar vertical members formed a screen that separated the Lady Chapel from the main volume.

The process of developing the cathedral design took from the time of Spence's first visit to the site, almost until the consecration in 1962, and certainly important decisions were taken after work was under way. Reference has already been made to the discussions of the architect and Bishop Gorton, and it is clear that a fruitful creative process was developed by these two, in conjunction with Provost Howard, who refers to his 'many years of close and constant contact' with Spence. Spence describes Gorton as a saintly man whose manner cast a strange, even bizarre, figure, but was 'surrounded by gusts of the Holy Spirit'—as the Archbishop of Canterbury said at his funeral. Spence also was a deeply religious man, Howard tells us, and in *Phoenix at Coventry* Spence tells of his personal dedication to the task with which he had been entrusted. Spence's passion for his work and commitment to the cause of architecture in which he believed, were products of a personality that was ever given to enthusiasms and causes, and their concomitant, opposition, dissent, and strife. It has been said of his years as President of the RIBA, for example (1958–60) that his sensitivity, and personal and emotional involvement, produced enemies as well as supporters, but nothing diverted him from the paths he had chosen. His task of creating his cathedral brought many difficulties of various kinds. He probably knew that often architects have won competitions to design a cathedral but not built them, and time and again he was filled with fears that it would never actually happen. The business of producing that work must now be outlined.

CONSTRUCTING AND COMMISSIONING

An architect does not simply design a building, and then leave the matter in the hands of others, but rather, is responsible for leading a team of professionals who are responsible for many different areas of concern, in the implementation of legal contracts and administrative procedures of all kinds. These areas include matters relating to materials, structural systems, building services, and, above all, cost. Cathedrals, ancient or modern, are ultimately produced by money and administrative organization.

From the production of his first (competition) design, Basil Spence worked with the eminent engineer Ove Arup, whose name has been associated with the most prestigious projects, and their designers, in modern British architecture. Arup later described his work as being that of making the architect's vision structurally possible. The structure, he wrote, should be subservient to the architecture, but the architect's design must not produce structural nonsense; and so the work of architect and structural engineer was one of close collaboration. The process of designing the vault was one Arup described as the architect's continual struggle to find a form that satisfied him, 'aided and abetted by the engineers'.

In the first years after the competition, Spence was busy not only with developing his design, but with securing its approval by the Royal Fine Art Commission, the Central Council for the Care of Churches, and Coventry's planning authority. He was wary of the RFAC, after Scott's fate, but there he had an ally in the form of Edward Maufe. They took two meetings (14 November, 12 December, 1951) to decide that his design was 'capable of resulting in a fine building'. Planning permission was obtained (9 January 1952), but the city council continued the opposition to the re-building that they had presented when the Cathedral Council had planned to build Scott's design. This opposition lasted for a long time. The objection was to the deployment of resources on such an 'unnecessary' building, when materials were badly needed for housing. Gorton readily agreed that housing should have priority: but the cathedral would employ materials and labour that were not of the kind used in house-building. The council advised them to wait ten years, and opposed the granting of a building licence. These were issued by the government, and were intended to restrain the construction industry, because of the problems of post-war material shortages.

In 1952 Spence consulted architect P. B. Chatwin, who had studied the history of the building of St Michael's. The condition of the ruins needed to be assessed, and remedial works were necessary. The crypts had become very damp, and the tops of the walls were exposed. Chatwin pointed out that some of the roof's lead had poured into the joints as natural grout; but much needed to be done. J. R. Deacon & Co. of Lichfield were contracted to make the walls and floors waterproof, with the instruction that their work would be considered truly successful if no visible effect of their efforts was left. This work (from August 1952) was interrupted when, for several days in September, it was thought that there was an unexploded bomb buried in the apse vestry ruins. Various other works were carried out in the old cathedral at this time (as the bells could not be swung, a keyboard was installed to produce a carillon; it was first used on Coronation Day, in 1953). Later works included the re-constructing of the Capper's Room. Spence produced a design in 1954, and it was finally dedicated in December 1957.

Also in 1952, Spence began visiting quarries in the area of Hollington, Staffordshire, and tenders were invited from various stone producers. The government's Building Research

Station later tested a wall of Hollington stone, and were involved in the production of an internal render whose specific constitution would produce the precise acoustic effect required. Samples of stone were tested at the University of Birmingham, for durability: the friability of Coventry's building stone was *not* to be repeated. Eventually, the stone was to be restricted to the outer-leaf of the walls, the acoustic-finished render being set on concrete blocks (6 in/152 mm), with mass-concrete cavity fill (the external stone *is* loadbearing, however, and 8 in/203 mm thick). A licence for initial building work was obtained in June 1952, and in July 1953 the all-important enabling legislation was passed, the Coventry Cathedral Act. In the following October, site-investigation tests were made. In May 1954 the indispensible building licence for the major works was finally obtained, and in September, six contractors were invited to tender for the first contract. In the autumn, the lowest tender was accepted, that of John Laing Construction. John Laing, founder of one of Britain's greatest construction companies, was a deeply religious man, and determined to be involved, if possible, in the building of the new cathedral. He was pleased to have won, but knew that this contract was only the beginning. Laing's site agent moved his caravan in, in February 1955. Already the site had been fenced, and the graveyard's contents were being removed. Though the site agent was briefly troubled by the ghostly monk, he and his company were shortly removing great quantities of earth and inserting reinforced-concrete bored piles (600, initially); a difficult operation was the construction of a large 'service-tunnel'. During this work, some foundations of the first cathedral were unearthed, to which reference has been made, on the western side. They were footings of what may have been small chapels or exedrae, of late construction (fifteenth-century) in the history of St Mary's. They were left exposed and visible, and still are. The monks' graveyard was also found, nearby. (See pp. 29, 30 and 33.)

On 30 November 1955, Neville Gorton, bishop since 1943, died after a sudden illness. He was buried in the cathedral ruins after a moving service at Holy Trinity. The first contract was complete early in 1956, enabling the foundation-stone to be laid by the Queen on 23 March. By this time, Laing's had won the second contract, to fix stone to the exterior of the lowest stage of the building; during these operations, a new bishop was appointed, Cuthbert K. N. Bardsley, who was enthroned in the ruins on 5 May 1956. Bardsley, who had served in various parishes in South London, strongly supported the cathedral design, and was eager to finish the work quickly. As the work of the second contract moved to completion, the third was announced. This—the nave, several chapels, refectory, verger's flat, etc.—was the most important. John Laing was anxious to win it, and with Spence's support, he did, much to his satisfaction. In November, a letter was sent by Laing's to each of their employees involved with the building, stressing the importance of their work, and that they were building a church that must last over a thousand years. The contract was signed on 13 December 1956 (recently they had signed to build Berkeley nuclear power station; the two projects were dubbed 'the power and the glory'). Donating this, and waiving fees for that, Laings gave considerable help to the cathedral. Several of their best craftsmen were moved from Carlisle, where they had been restoring its cathedral— another gothic victim of poor stone.

Of course, there were problems. The quarry originally contracted had failed to supply the stone required, and a new one, that of Stanton and Bettany, was found. Choice of quarry is important; one reason is that much preparatory work is done there, with cutting and sizing, as the newly-cut stone is still soft, until exposed to the air. In May 1956, a new firm of quantity surveyors (those who organize the measurement of materials and work, and control the project's economics), Messrs. Reynolds and Young, were appointed.

Unlike most cathedral building projects, the whole area of wall was raised at once: in September 1957, the walls were 24 feet/7.31 metres high [though dimensions are here given metric equivalents, the cathedral, and the subsequent cathedrals at Liverpool (Metropolitan) and Clifton, were designed in Imperial units]. Half way through 1958, 71 piles were sited where the porch was to be. In August, Provost Howard resigned. He had stated his intention of retiring when the reconstruction was well advanced; he had been at the cathedral since 1933. In September, Harold C. N. Williams was appointed. Williams had rebuilt his church of St Mary, Southampton, after wartime destruction. 1958 saw the transference of worship from the chapels in the ruins to a new Chapel of the Cross in the new cathedral's basement. In December the walls had reached c.60 feet/18.28 metres. In September 1959 the Lady Chapel's roof trusses were concreted, and much of the stonework of the baptistery window was fixed (completed 1 March 1960). In October 1959 the first of the fourteen internal columns was fixed. These were cast in Bridport, then glued together on site with Araldite, post-tensioned using four steel strands, and fixed into position on bronze pins. In December a contract relating to the (independently administered) Chapel of Unity was signed. In 1960, the covering of the roofs with copper began (completed April 1961), and in May of that year, a contract was signed concerned with the building of the Guild Chapel (which became the Chapel of Industry).

At this time, the task of installing the many art works, fittings, furnishings and decorations was under way. As with the story of the building's construction, the typescript account written by Captain N. T. Thurston, Secretary of the Reconstruction Committee, provides a wealth of detailed information on their commissioning and production: this document forms part of the cathedral's archives.

From very early in his design process, Spence decided that his cathedral would be as a 'casket' filled with many 'jewels'— in the form of works of contemporary religious art of the finest quality obtainable. In his first 'vision' of the future building, he refers to seeing the altar through bodies of the saints, and in his 'pre-dentistry' dream, we saw him experiencing the effect of beautiful lighting from the windows at the side of the nave, and a great tapestry. When producing his competition design, Spence decided that if he won, he would ask Graham Sutherland to design the tapestry, and he allowed £30,000 for this work in his competition cost assessment. Sutherland was approached in December 1951. In September 1952, Spence went to Robin Darwin, principal of the Royal College of Art, in connection with the nave's side windows. Laurence Lee (head of the department of stained glass) with Keith New and Geoffrey Clarke, were chosen to produce the windows, being employed by the college. The contract with the Royal College was signed on 17 October. In December, money was donated from Germany for the production of the Chapel of Unity's windows, and in the same month the name of John Hutton was recommended to the committee by Spence, as the person most suitable for producing the engraved figures on the great glass screen. Hutton had worked with Maufe at Guildford, and on the air force memorial, Runnymede (inaugurated October 1953) also by Maufe. Hutton and Provost Howard worked together on the subject material, which was approved in 1953. In March 1953, the tapestry wall's 'move' was approved, giving greater depth to the space in front of it (50 feet/15.24 metres more), and making its 'reredos' into that of the Lady Chapel. In the following December, Spence, Howard and Gorton visited Sutherland in Kent to see his first cartoon. Gorton contributed suggestions and criticisms concerned with the subject-matter, and allegedly delayed the artist, who in all did many sketches and studies, but only three actual schemes. His re-workings had to take account of such things as the changes of internal tonality, caused by the adoption of white rough-cast, rather than stone, as the interior finish. The second cartoon was submitted to the committee in January 1955. From the beginning, Spence wanted the tapestry to be woven by the Edinburgh Tapestry Company, but various problems, including delays with the production of the final cartoon (or maquette) and the technique of production (in panels, or whole?), militated against this. Sutherland went to Pinton Frères of Felletin, near Aubusson, France, where the production was directed by Marie Cuttoli, who had done such work for many of the leading modern French artists.

In July 1955, John Piper agreed to design the stained glass for the great baptistery window (which was made by Patrick Reyntiens). In the same month, the Reconstruction Committee accepted Spence's suggestions that Sir Jacob Epstein be approached concerning the figure of St Michael, which was to be made for fixing to the outside of the cathedral. At first, the committee was uncertain, as Epstein was 'controversial'; but his *Madonna and Child* in London's Cavendish Square (1951–52), made a strong impression on Gorton in 1954, as did the Birmingham *Lucifer* (1944–45) on Spence in the same year. At this time, Epstein was working on his *Majestas*, or Christ in Majesty (1953–57), which was a part of the reconstructed Llandaff Cathedral, Wales, another victim of wartime bombing.

The foundation stone, laid in March 1956, was one of the first works of Ralph Beyer to be installed: his inscriptional carvings are to be found on stones throughout the cathedral. It was Nikolaus Pevsner who first suggested to Spence that this artist be commissioned; Beyer was the son of a distinguished German scholar who had studied Early Christian inscriptions, and Ralph Beyer's principal work was to be the Tablets of the Word. In July 1956, the first six—out of ten—nave windows were completed, and early in the new year, 1957, Spence,

The angel in the Chapel of Christ in Gethsemane, a detail from the relief on the northern wall by Steven Sykes.

Howard, and Bishop Bardsley visited Epstein and, with some surprise, found the work much advanced; photographs of it removed the doubts that had been expressed in the Reconstruction Committee. In September of this year, Sutherland's third, and final, tapestry cartoon was submitted to the committee—but almost immediately he was revising it. In December, the restored Capper's Room was dedicated. It contained a tapestry of the arms of the Capper's Company, woven by the Edinburgh Tapestry Company; by this time, the weaving of Sutherland's tapestry had been fully organized in France, where the cartoon was sent in February 1958. In the following June, the plaster casting of Epstein's sculpture was complete, and the bronze head of St Michael was approved in March 1959; the sculptor died in the following August. Spence had been introduced to Margaret Traherne, a stained glass artist who used the medium of thick glass, set in concrete, in abstract design. Spence considered that this was an appropriate method of glazing the Chapel of Unity, and in modifying his design

Details from the Swedish windows (the work of Einar Forseth): LEFT: English missionaries taking the Christian faith to Sweden.
RIGHT: Emblems of the British nations, and other devices.

for that chapel, produced long, thin slits, to be filled with Traherne's work; she submitted her designs in September 1959.

In 1960 Basil Spence was knighted (all of the designers of Britain's major cathedrals, since Wren, have been knighted, except Pearson of Truro and Bentley of Westminster); by now success at Coventry must have seemed assured. The pace of work, in the production and installation of Spence's 'jewels', was accelerating. Throughout 1960 teams of embroiderers (including a railway fitter at Rugby, and dancers at the Theatre Royal, Drury Lane) worked on the 1000 kneelers, that were produced to six separate designs. In May, Steven Sykes unveiled his design for the Gethsemane Chapel relief. This was to be set on the rear wall of the chapel originally referred to as the Chapel of the Resurrection; it was to be made in *ciment fondu*. In June, Epstein's great sculpture was delivered and fixed in place. Einar Forseth, who did the mosaics in the Golden Room of Stockholm Town Hall, was a Swedish artist determined to contribute to Coventry Cathedral. He persuaded Spence to accept his works, and Swedish officials to raise the money, in Sweden, to pay for them (about £5,000). His design for the floor mosaic in the Chapel of Unity was accepted in November 1960 (and later, five stained glass windows were added to the Swedish gift). In December, by way of Beirut and Manchester, a boulder arrived from near Bethlehem. Spence's idea was that a large rock from Iona be used for the cathedral font, but his friend Frankland Dark, an architect working in the Middle East, arranged to procure one from the birthplace of Jesus, and, with the help of the British ambassador in Beirut, and Laing's financial assistance, it was brought to Coventry. Ralph Beyer made the hollow in the top to hold water; it was first used on 24 June 1962.

In January 1961, Ralph Beyer began work on the Tablets of the Word, biblical texts cut in large stone panels in the nave. They were carved *in situ*, and not in the studio. Following the completion of the baptistery window's stonework (March 1960) the installation of the Piper and Reyntiens glass began, in May 1961; it was completed by the end of October. In this year, a group of German students arrived in Coventry from the organization *Aktion Sühnezeichen* (Action for Reconciliation). The students constructed the cathedral's International Centre, which was dedicated in April 1962. Early in 1962, Geoffrey Clarke submitted his design for the altar cross, to be set on the high altar, and the construction of the flèche, to be sited on the roof at the southern end, was begun.

The weaving of Graham Sutherland's tapestry had begun in 1959, and time and again the artist had visited the weavers to examine their work. His last visit was made in December 1961, and the task was completed on 18 February 1962. An airline provided a special plane that flew the rolled tapestry directly to Coventry from France, in March. The final cost was £20,000. Just prior to that, the sculptor Elisabeth Frink had been commissioned to cast a bronze eagle, which held the lectern; she also produced various other works for this part of the cathedral. One of the last artworks to be commissioned were the six candlesticks that stand beside the high altar. Made by Hans Coper, they are of thrown pottery. At 8.30 on the morning of 26 April, an RAF helicopter lowered the flèche carefully onto the cathedral roof. Two days later, Geoffrey Clarke's 'flying cross' was set upon the flèche by the same method. Many referred to these procedures as a gimmick or stunt; in fact, it was simply the cheapest way that the tasks could be achieved.

On Friday 25 May 1962, the cathedral was consecrated. The Archbishop of Canterbury gave the address on the text: 'The latter glory of this house shall be greater than the former, saith the Lord of Hosts: and in this place will I give peace' (Haggai Ch. 2 v. 9).

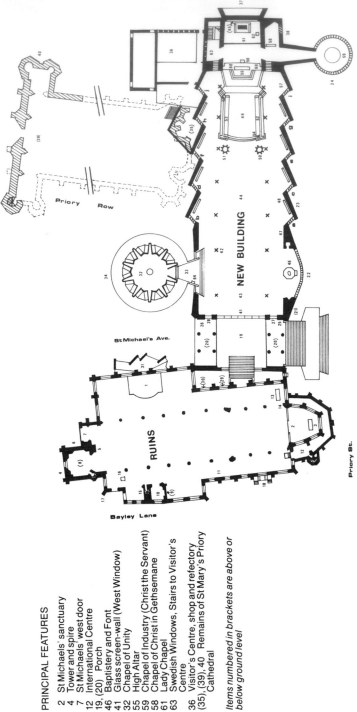

PRINCIPAL FEATURES

- 2 St Michaels' sanctuary
- 4 Tower and spire
- 7 St Michaels' west door
- 12 International Centre
- 19, (20) Porch
- 46 Baptistery and Font
- 41 Glass screen-wall (West Window)
- 32 Chapel of Unity
- 55 High Altar
- 59 Chapel of Industry (Christ the Servant)
- 58 Chapel of Christ in Gethsemane
- 61 Lady Chapel
- 63 Swedish Windows, Stairs to Visitor's Centre
- 36 Visitor's Centre, shop and refectory
- (35), (39), 40 Remains of St Mary's Priory Cathedral

Items numbered in brackets are above or below ground level

Chapter Six

A WALK AROUND COVENTRY CATHEDRAL

THE RUINS AND EXTERIORS

WE MUST BEGIN in the ruined St Michael's, for this place is the source of the whole meaning and experience of Coventry Cathedral as it is now. We stand not in a medieval church, but in a place that has been fashioned, by modern destruction and re-creation, as a different, very special, public place. The ruins as they have been presented, are not the place that visitors knew before the Second World War; and yet we can know the medieval church through them and by way of them. The ruined cathedral is physically, and experientially, part of the whole, and as such it is regarded and used by the cathedral authorities, and this unity was the work of the architect. Today, it is an *agora*, a public meeting-place, a common space; it is the equivalent of the *piazza* of an Italian town, or the *forum* of Roman cities. In the middle of the northern outer-aisle, a permanent stage is set against the outer-wall (numbered (1) on the plan opposite). This was constructed in 1949, and the modern tradition of religious drama was begun; it was a use of religious art that recalls Coventry's medieval plays. This stage, and drama, adds something of the qualities of an ancient open-air theatre. The ruins are not just roof-less, they are opened-out space. Because the building is wide (north–south axis: 130 feet/39.62 metres) and the high clerestory and colonnade are gone, the walls are low, in proportion to the width, they do not *contain*, as most buildings do, they do not limit, define or create a three-dimensional volume, for above, the space flies away to the infinity of the sky. On the morning after the building's destruction, Provost Howard felt that the *new* building was larger than the old; but to me the ruins seem small, and probably because they have little containment of space. The 'sky's vault' (Spence described it in such terms) dwarfs the ruined remnants and the new porch's canopy also makes the gothic walls seem puny; on his first visit, Spence experienced 'delicate enclosure'. For a building to be big, it must bind space into a whole.

The new *agora* is completely unlike St Michael's of old, of the late Middle Ages: this was a building divided and sub-divided into different spaces with different functions and different users (guild chapels, guild rooms, chantry chapels, screened sanctuary, etc.). Today, these screens and divisions are gone, all except a low, simple wall, that separates off the space of the apse (or sanctuary, which was re-furnished, etc., in the 1930s) (2).

The ruined St Michael's is an embodiment and a symbol of the futile destruction of war, and thereby of the religious doctrines of death and sacrifice that are the heart of the Christian religion. This symbolic nature, we have seen (pp. 74–8), emerged spontaneously and naturally, and was then incorporated or re-presented, as part of the eventual whole. In this way, the old St Michael's was transformed into something that is unique in this country's religious architecture. In the apse we see the famous Altar of Rubble (3), set up soon after the cathedral's burning by incendiary bombs on the night of 14 November 1940 (p. 78), and behind it, the Charred Cross, made from burned medieval timbers from the old cathedral roof; on the wall behind that are the incised words *Father Forgive*. For many this is a very moving sight today as before when memories of war's destruction were fresh. Each Friday at noon, the liturgy of reconciliation is offered in this place, and the altar is now the Altar of Reconciliation. Its prayers refer to the hatred and rivalries that oppose nations, races, and classes, and the covetous desires of nations and people, to possess; the response is 'Father forgive'.

Beneath our feet there are paving-stones. In the 1950s and early 1960s, there was grass here and pathways. These separated, in some measure, the eastern portion of the ruined church (the apse, etc.) from the western (the stage—arena). But grass proved unsuitable, and hence the pavings: in these are set two lines, in cobble-stones. They mark the east–west axes of the tower, and of the western entrance-porch.

The Tower

The gothic building that perished in 1940 was created by building a tower at west (from 1373 to mid-1390s; spire by c.1433) (4), which was raised against an existing thirteenth-century nave, and then, slightly later, beginning a new church, from the east (the apse) on a different alignment (see p. 52). This all created what Nikolaus Pevsner called the 'great and undeniably painful anomaly of the church'—different axes and oddly-related volumes, and structures. One of the largest of all English parish churches (which it was before 1918), its floor area was 24,000 square feet/2,229.6 square metres, its total overall length c.240 feet/73.15 metres.

John Harvey calls St Michael's tower and spire 'a work of genius fit to rank ... with the Wonders of the World', and refers to the 'sophisticated eclecticism' of Perpendicular archi-tecture, which it demonstrates. From the ground to the base of the octagon stage it has been measured as 130 feet/39.62 metres, the octagon is c.30 feet/9.14 metres high, the spire c.125 feet/38.10 metres, and the whole is c.295 feet/89.91 metres. It always stood open on three sides, of course, but now is open on the fourth, and course-marks in the stonework of the eastern face show how it was built up against an earlier nave, to which it fitted symmetrically, only to have a new, wider, higher, roof placed awkwardly beside it. On this eastern face a statue of St Michael for long stood (5); now a tablet recounts the words of the prophet Haggai Ch. 2, v. 9, *The latter glory of this house shall be greater than the former ....* Today's tower owes much to the 1880s restoration of John Oldrid Scott (see pp. 62–7). Old engravings show the great structure cocooned in a vast web of timber scaffolding. Outside, on the north face of the lower stages, we see small panels of lighter coloured, worn stone, set in a sea of nineteenth-century masonry (6); these belong to that small area of the old structure, it seems, that may have been sound when Scott worked on it. He found the building in a very ruinous condition (some unrestored buttresses to the south (17) and north aisles—at west—give a hint, possibly, of this decrepitude). The shallow western entrance-porch that adjoins the tower's north side (7) is now bereft of its doors. It has a miniature lierne-vault (unrestored) of considerable charm; about five of the bosses have carving whose forms can still be made out. The exquisite under-tower vault (8) was built by J. O. Scott in the late 1880s; it replaces a destroyed medieval vault (see p. 63). The view from the tower's octagon-stage is strongly recommended: the steps require physical fitness, however.

From the tower, we can look down on the ruins, and see the whole form and extent of St Michael's. It will be seen that the top of the old walls have been capped with concrete (in the 1950s), strengthening them for the future. From here, we can see into the ring of vestries, around the outside of the apse (12), or rather, the new facility the restored vestries contain, with their copper roofs. The other great copper roof is that of the new building: the nave, porch, and baptistery roof (as that between the Chapel of Unity and baptistery is sometimes called), with its flèche. The green of the copper (Foreman Coppersmith Frank McGilley laid some 35,000 square feet/ 3,251.5 square metres of it) contrasts with the pink stone and slate cladding of the walls. The projecting canopy looks very different from here, and the two stone slab-like walls support-ing it (transverse to the new cathedral axis), look particularly effective. The flèche, made by the firm of J. Starkie Gardner, is nearly 90 feet/27.43 metres high, and was designed by Ove Arup. It was lowered onto the roof by RAF helicopter, and fixed into place, on 26 April 1962. The 'flying cross' that surmounts it was similarly installed two days later. It was designed by Geoffrey Clarke, and made of cast aluminium alloy, and is 10 feet/3.04 metres high and 8 feet/2.43 metres across. RAF Operations 'Rich Man', 'Needle' and 'Camel' were named from the gospel of the day of 26 April, St Matthew Ch. 19, v. 24. From here we can also see the top of the outer walls of the nave, and the other churches of Coventry (Holy Trinity, St John's, Bablake, and the spire of the Grey-friars (Christ Church)), west and south-west. Above and behind we see the octagon-stage of the tower itself (p. 56), and the fine pairs of diverging flying buttresses that rise up from the outer pinnacles to the upper-octagon.

The Nave and Chapels of the Ruins

Back on the ground, the bases of the arcade's columns, the width between them, and the fragment that remains high on the nave's western wall, give some idea of the size of the columns, panelled spandrels, clerestory windows, and the great low roofs, which have all gone. Surviving windows show examples of the complexity of reticulations that the acres of Perpendicular tracery once possessed, and those in the eastern bays of the northern outer-aisle, behind and to the right of the stage (1), had pierced tracery (i.e. window) flanked by blind tracery (mostly cut away, now) all enveloped by a large window-arch. Several walls show evidence of stairs and stair-cases, by which the private guild-rooms and chapels were entered. Behind the stage we see the remains of a north porch, which had a room above. The Cappers Guild still exists, and they have a room that was created by Basil Spence, in the 1950s, on top of the south porch (9). The south porch is now a memorial chapel to the third bishop, M. G. Haigh (1931 42), and is closed off by a glass screen. This is the oldest part of the building (late thirteenth-century) and gave access to the thirteenth-century nave (10). Around the walls we see the 'Hallowing Places', words carved in tablets of slate. They are prayers of blessing upon aspects of everyday modern life ('Hallowed be thy name in recreation. God be in my limbs and in my leisure', 'Hallowed be thy name in the arts. God be in my senses and in my creating'.) Along the south wall we come to a large stone statue, *Ecce Homo* ('Behold the Man', St John Ch. 19, v. 5). This rendering of Christ before Pilate was carved by Jacob Epstein in 1934–35 (11). For long, its harsh forms proved unacceptable as a depiction of Jesus, and only after several attempts by Anglican clergy to find a home for it, was it brought to Coventry (1970s). It reflects the sculptor's early interests in the forms of African and Polynesian art, which he acquired in his years in Paris, and contrasts sharply with his later religious works. Weathering has softened the forms of this Easter Island-like Christ. To those sympathetic, his gross-ness perhaps expresses the injustice of his treatment, and all such bondage; for others, it is hard to see the Saviour in this ugliness (p. 177).

At the end of the south chancel aisle, beside the apse, steps lead under a canopy, composed of jarring diagonals, to the International Centre for Reconciliation, in the former vestries (12). This route is exactly that taken by the 1940 fire, which, having consumed the organ in the adjacent Mercer's Chapel, burned the vestries one by one; but to this place in 1962 came members of *Aktion Sühnezeichen* from Germany, and built the centre now housed there. Beside this entrance is the grave of

Bishop Gorton (1943–55). In the north chancel aisle stands the weathered-green memorial to H. W. Yeatman–Biggs, the first bishop (1918–22) (13). Unveiled in 1925, this was one of the last works of Sir Hamo Thorneycroft (1850–1925), a leading member of the *fin de siécle* 'New Sculpture', and of the Arts and Crafts movement. After the cathedral's burning, pictures show this recumbent effigy seeming to float on a sea of rubble. It was restored and re-set in 1954. In the first part of this century, several fine works in this form were produced, including the Lever tombs at Port Sunlight (1913, 1925), the Elphinstone memorial, Aberdeen (erected 1926), and the memorial to the XVIth Earl of Derby at Liverpool Cathedral (1929); it is a form readily producing that quality of *gravitas* possessed by so many Renaissance tombs. The bishop holds a model of the cathedral on his breast. Above, beside the chancel arch, there stands a life-size statue of Christ, who looks down with hands held open (14). It was originally modelled in clay, between the wars, by a seventeen-year-old schoolboy, later killed in the war. It was installed in the mid-1940s.

If we return to the western portion of the southern aisle, we see, in the former Dyer's Chapel, a survivor of the many monuments that St Michael's contained, from the sixteenth, seventeenth, and eighteenth centuries. It commemorates Dame Mary Bridgeman and Mrs Eliza Samwell (1724), of whom there are medallion-portraits (15). Nearby, a pinnacle from the parapet has been re-built on the ground to commemorate the visit of King George VI to the ruins on 16 November 1940 (16). The small doorway to the east of the Dyer's Chapel leads onto Bayley Lane. Looking west, we see the contrast of an unrestored diagonal-buttress of the south aisle with the tower's angle-buttresses (17). Walking east down Bayley Lane we come to the outside of the south porch (or Haigh Chapel) (10), with its early cusped plate-tracery, now filled with glass. Beyond the porch, outside the southern chancel aisle, we see the entrance made into the Dyer's Chapel in 1750 (18). At the bottom of Bayley Lane we come to Priory Street, and here we get a good view of the apse, International Centre, etc. (12). Prior to the 1880s restoration, the vestries had lost most of their buttresses, and the apse its pinnacles (see pp. 62–3): the 1849 painting by David Gee, in the nearby Herbert Art Gallery and Museum, shows one stage in the church's process of decline. Frith's photograph, taken from this point after the restoration (p. 58) shows the hard, crisp forms of newly-cut stone (and

The porch which connects old and new cathedrals looking up St Michael's Avenue from Priory St.

reminds us of the contemporary *fin de siècle* gothic of such as Temple Moore). Proceeding north up Priory Street we pass the probable site of the palace where Coventry's medieval bishops lived; turning left (west) we ascend the steps (of St Michael) which leads to Spence's porch (19), the great concrete canopy which bridges St Michael's Avenue, and links the old and the new, the cathedral destroyed and the cathedral risen again. The porch and its columns and supporting walls surely produce one of the most successful parts of the new building,

Jacob Epstein's St Michael and the Devil from below.

and the space they create is one of the most exciting. It is, of
course, a cross-axis, giving several views. We can look up into
it, from the bottom of St Michael's steps, or down into it, from
the ruins. Some find the columns too slender, but perhaps this
reaction is due to familiarity: perhaps we are too used to the
massive medieval bulk of Durham and Gloucester. Others
object to concrete columns being clad in stone: but this view is
the result of what we must call a particular architectural
ideology. Just before the top, however, Spence curiously
chooses to reveal the true nature of the porch's supports—the
concrete is exposed. The porch's central concrete shell has sets
of three transverse shells set beside it (20): in the earlier schemes
(e.g. exterior perspective of July 1952) these were pointed in
elevation, resembling small pitched-roofs. Their eventual

shape is that of inverted channels, which have the somewhat harsher form of an extruded metal section or length of sheet-piling. The scale and spaciousness of the porch was inspired by the great size of Gerona Cathedral, Spain, and Spence was also impressed by the vast porch at Albi Cathedral, France.

The East Side of the Cathedral

St Michael's steps project outward to form a platform from which we can view the sculpture that gives them their name: Jacob Epstein's *St Michael and the Devil* (21). Epstein (1880–1959) was commissioned following the suggestion of Basil Spence in 1955 (see p. 113). The bronze-casting of the work, by Morris Singer of South Lambeth, London (who restored the Yeatman-Biggs memorial) cost £7,800. It was unveiled by Lady Epstein on 24 June 1960; on this occasion, Bishop Bardsley called the Devil 'a man, fallen man, as we see him today, frustrated, disillusioned . . .' This work should perhaps be seen in comparison with the 1944–45 *Lucifer*, at Birmingham City Art Galleries, for this Miltonic Satan, like the Coventry Michael, stands erect, overshadowed by great wings, reminding us of Lucifer's original angelic nature. Lucifer's *contrapposto*, and hands held forward, contrast with Michael's outstretched arms and legs, and lance held upward in victorious gesture. Beneath Michael's left foot, the Devil lies in chains; the two figures do not quite touch. Michael's clothing is blown sideways by the exertions of recent conflict; the Devil is naked, wrapped only in the bondage of his self made destruction. His bulging eyes look upward with grim resignation; but Michael's gaze is more distant, and seems to have a quality of sadness, or pity, as though possessing the knowledge that such struggle is far from over. The sculpture weighs over 4 tons/4.06 tonnes. Michael is 19 feet 6 inches/5.944 metres high, the Devil measures 11 feet 3 inches/3.429 metres long. The top of Michael's head is just under 30 feet/9.14 metres from the ground.

Proceeding north, we see the outside of the baptistery window (22). The stone was fixed by Foreman Mason Harold Ratcliffe, with other masons; the topmost stone (height of 75 feet/22.86 metres) was set on 1 March 1960. Most characteristic are the window's deep triangular-sectioned horizontals. Beneath the baptistery window, the stone is scabbled to produce the effect of vermiculation (as found also on the west side). Beyond the baptistery are the famous saw-toothed

ABOVE, RIGHT and LEFT: Two of the door handles, which include cherubic sculptures, by Jacob Epstein.

windows of the nave (23). Their long vertical mullions, and short transoms, produce an effect recalling Perpendicular tracery. Further north, we see the Chapel of Industry, begun in November 1960. Its lower stage was designed as the Chapter House (24). It is composed of many single-piece pre-cast concrete verticals, clad in green Westmorland slate. This chapel compositionally balances St Michael's apse, to its south, and the Chapel of Unity, to the west, on the transverse axis.

The Porch
Returning to the porch, beside the south-eastern door, we see the foundation stone, laid 23 March 1956; it weighs 1 ton/1.01 tonne (25). High on the wall opposite, an inscription commemorates the life of Sir Basil Spence. Beside the south-western door, there is a stone taken from Lichfield Cathedral, laid to commemorate Coventry's long association with Lichfield, in its ancient diocese (26) (unveiled June 1958, both stones carved by Ralph Beyer). These doors (27, 28; by which we normally enter and leave the new building) and those beneath the engraved panels, have handles in the form of delicate

OPPOSITE: The exterior of the Chapel of Industry (Christ the Servant), looking north, showing the slate-clad concrete mullions that rise to full height.

The exterior of the Chapel of Unity, from the former churchyard, beside St Michael's Avenue.

cherubic figures, the work of Epstein, and originally intended for the Convent of the Holy Child of Jesus, Cavendish Square, London. Opposite, to the right of the staircase leading up to the ruins, we find the entrances to the medieval crypts, now chapels. That to our right (30) is a crypt built as part of the church constructed at the end of the thirteenth century (see p. 51). It has rib vaults raised on two octagonal columns, set laterally (many of the Priory's monastic buildings were raised on vaults similar to these). In 1940, it was used as an air raid shelter, and here terrified citizens huddled, while above, the

The Chapel of Unity, No. 11 Priory Row, and the Visitor's Centre refectory, seen from St Michael's tower.

great stones and timbers crashed down on them (see pp. 72–3). Later, it was a choir practice room, but now it is the Chapel of the Cross, and contains a modern free-standing altar in its south-western bay, an illuminated cross by Geoffrey Clarke, an ikon from Stalingrad Cathedral, and a large gothic oak chair, that looks like a fragment from St Michael's ancient stalls. To the east is a slightly later crypt, now the Wyley Chapel (29). It has two bays, running north–south, rib-vaulted, with the southern bay somewhat truncated (against the southern wall is the modern altar, beside it, a medieval piscina). A modern carving on the west wall depicts Christ, a serpent, and angels. The chapel commemorates the Wyley family.

The West Side of the Cathedral

Continuing up St Michael's Avenue, the jagged assymmetrical forms of Spence's bookshop—and its grey granite stone—(31) contrasts with the regular geometry of the Chapel of Unity, and its green slate cladding (32). The siting and form of the chapel were crucial (see p. 102): Spence likened it to a crusader's tent, but it can as easily resemble some apparatus for space travel. The glass funnel which leads people into it is largely clear glass, as is part of the nave-wall beside it (33): we can thus see through it entirely, or into the cathedral. The area west of the Chapel of Unity (34), and all around the buildings, were landscaped with great care (in March 1962 a semi-mature sycamore tree was transported from Berkhamstead and re-planted), and certainly the whole ambience of the space that was created around and between the buildings, old and new, is very lovely. Bordering it, on the site of Coventry's first cathedral, is Priory Row, a terrace of pleasant Georgian houses. 1950s photographs show No. 11 (like No. 7, owned by the cathedral) burnt-out and ruinous after bombing. To its east, beside the Visitor's Centre (36) and the modern cathedral's western wall, we can look down to see the footings of what are thought to be fifteenth-century chapels, added to the Priory church's eastern extremity (35) (see pp. 33–4). Adjacent to these early remains is the entrance to the Refectory, gift-shop, and Visitor's Centre. A passage through the refectory leads out onto a terrace raised above an area of hard-landscape (37). To the west and north-west of this point, the Priory's monastic buildings once stood: dorter, rere-dorter, Chapter House, and farmery (see pp. 30, 38).

The North End

From here we can look up at the cathedral's northern wall. It is cliff-like, without openings, and has vast undecorated sur-faces—but is very effective and satisfying. At each corner, battered buttresses ascend from bottom to top, uninterrupted by weatherings or a string-course. They are set diagonally, but with their outer-face square with the main façade. By walking east towards the Chapel of Industry, we see the outside of the Lady Chapel's east wall, with its grid of tall strip-windows. Beneath, a group of obliquely-set mullions form a grille across a window-opening; they rise up and die into a bevelled lintel, the whole producing a complexity of acutely-angled surfaces. This is the outside of the window of the Gethsemane Chapel, whose canted mullions (aided by a discreet electric light) produce the mosaic's hidden light-source (38). At this end, everything is canted, raked, battered, bevelled, or otherwise diagonal. Only the lowest (basement) windows contrast, with their totally square penetration of the walls. The success of these northern elevations owes much to the architect's exploitation of the inherent qualities of the material, Hollington stone, which has been fixed with great precision and care. In this use of material (and even in the design) the resulting work is suggestive of the turn-of-the-century Arts and Crafts movement. Hopefully, the stones will remain hard and sharp for a long time, though some, in the lowest courses, have spalled already. (Concerning the stone, etc., see p. 109–110.)

This north wall (which would have been pierced by the Lady Chapel's rear windows in Spence's first scheme (p. 107)) displays a large cross, in relief. This is the *cross potent and quadrate*, which is found on the 'carpet page' of the Lichfield Gospels (dated 730), and is Celtic in origin. In heraldry it is known as the 'Cross of St Chad' (see p. 8), and formed part of the diocesan arms which are thought to have originated in the time of Roger de Clinton (bishop 1129–48). When Coventry's modern diocese was founded (1918) this cross became part of its arms (though Coventry's cross is not *dimidiated* like Lichfield's, i.e. subdivided by a vertical line, see p. 181). Though acquired very recently, in terms of the history of Midlands' Christianity, Coventry lacked no restraint in its use of the cross, which is carved here, inset there, and printed everywhere. From here we can see a zany three-dimensional version surmounting the Chapel of Industry. At times it seems there are more representations of this cross in the modern buildings than there are of the Cross of Nails or the Charred Cross — which are authentically and uniquely Coventry's own.

The Priory's West Front

Returning to Priory Row, and proceeding west along it, we pass Holy Trinity church on the left. Then on the right, hidden between trees and buildings, are the lowest courses of the Priory church's west front, excavated in 1856 (39); this structure has been dated late-thirteenth century (see pp. 29 ff.). Moving north from the road we can make out the base of the

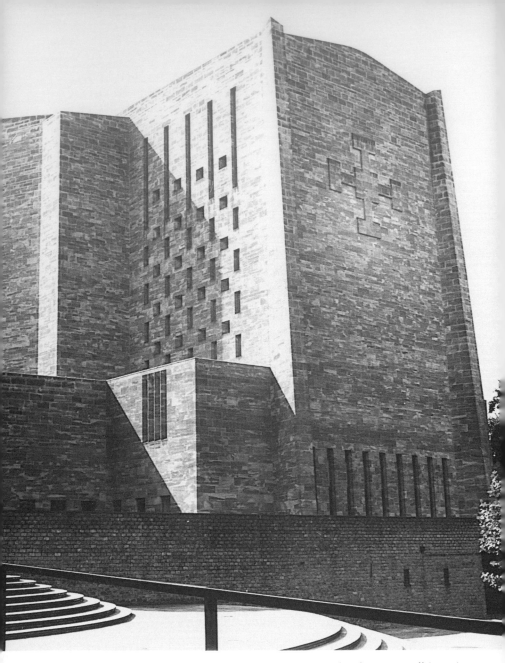

The northern end of the new building, showing the Lady Chapel's eastern wall (centre), beneath which is the projecting Chapel of Christ in Gethsemane and the blank northern wall (right) inside which the great tapestry is fixed.

south-west tower (with its remains of a spiral staircase), then
the western end of the south nave aisle, the central nave aisle
(the west door was here) and then the north aisle. A nineteenth-century building stands on the site of the north-western
tower (40). We see the remains of three piers of the southern
colonnade, their shafts cut through like moulding-diagrams in
an architectural text-book (see plan p. 30). If we proceed west,
turn right, along Trinity Street past the modern shops and then
right again into a small alley, we can see on our left a
nineteenth-century building whose lowest masonry courses are
surely the foundations of the Priory church's north-west tower
(see engraving p. 35). By returning to Trinity Street and then
proceeding right, down the street called New Buildings, we
approach the area where the Priory's mill and dye-works
stood; the kitchen and frater was slightly to the south. By
turning right and ascending Hill Top (to the right of which the
cathedral's youth hostel, J. F. Kennedy House, is situated) we
return to Priory Row.

THE NEW CATHEDRAL'S INTERIOR

The Nave

Basil Spence conceived of a new cathedral, sited to the north of
the ruined St Michael's, from which the altar (set at north)
could be seen through the bodies of the saints (p. 98). From the
former north chancel aisle, in the ruins, we look down through
the open gothic portal (former window): we see the bodies of
the saints, and angels, in the great screen wall (41); but to see
the altar it is normally necessary to descend and enter. Inside,
the building is very light—the southern glass screen wall makes
it so—and the space is very wide and high and open. The
southern portion of the nave (real compass directions are used
in this account) is generally clear of chairs, and normally an
open central 'aisle' proceeds to the liturgical area. From here
we readily experience the space that the architect has created.
The majestic figure of Christ is seen from beyond the altar, its
eyes fixing us with a powerful gaze that bridges distance. To
the right, the shower of colours from a large stained glass
window attract and, opposite that, a wide glass passageway
(33) leads into an intimate space that here we can only see in

part. These two, the baptistery, and Chapel of Unity (32) opposite, set up a strong transverse axis. The key to the nature of this space lies in the ambivalence that was surely evident from the ruins, where we began: the glass screen wall. It was intended to link, to open up and expose old to new, new to old. It does; it joins, and yet it divides more surely than any masonry wall, for unlike such, it acts as a mirror—sometimes in both directions—but this also, it does partially: from inside we see the sky, and from outside, the reflection of the sky (at night, reflections and glass disappear, as with one of today's buildings clad in solar-control glass). Its great transparency floods light in, which strangely damages the visual effects and tonalities of the building. It does for the containment of space what the loss of roofs did for St Michael's: each is a building composed of five planes, rather than the usual six. The ruins' 'delicate enclosure' has been re-created in the new.

Spence's early experiences of space involved dark, enclosed, womb-like places (p. 98): but there is little that is womb-like at Coventry, except the medieval crypts, and possibly the Chapel of Unity. Vital to the architect's ordering of space (large, as a unity, despite the small overall length (270 feet/82.29 metres): decreasing width produces illusionistic elongation) are the rows of cruciform columns that 'descend' from the 'vault' (42) (see pp. 100, 103, construction details, p. 112). The vault is 70 feet/21.33 metres from the floor, the nave is between 80 feet/ 24.38 metres and 85 feet/25.90 metres wide. Many have criticized Spence for indulging in this pseudo-structure, considering it a lamentable lapse into thinly-disguised Gothic Revivalism. But with no internal spatial 'punctuation', the nave might feel lifeless and amorphous (see also p. 100). The decreasing width of the columns (34 in/863 cm to 17 in/ 432 cm) is odd, and reminds one of the awful black tapered legs found on every 1950s coffee-table. The bronze shoes and square pin, on which each column stands (the latter $2\frac{1}{2}$ in/ 63.5 mm square) seems (like the exposed concrete core on the porch columns) to reveal a need, on the part of Spence, to openly display the 'underlying truth' of the structure, though, as Ove Arup wrote: 'It would be absurd to contend, as some architectural critics are apt to do, that the design of a cathedral should grow out of structural necessity.'

Spence tried several alternative versions of his vault before designing the present one (p. 106); it is made up of panels composed of over 28,700 slats of Sitka spruce, whose frames fit together to form a continuous web, with wooden 'ribs'. Clearly, the final result is like a gothic vault, and yet the whole thing has an absurd element: the ribs fly off from the columns, but miss the columns of the opposite side; they stop mid-air, for the whole vault is simply sliced-off at the sides, and by a *straight* cut (the walls, beside the vault are zig-zagged). Even on Lincoln's 'crazy vault' the ribs come to rest on a pier (had Spence been looking at ribs in Prague?); *this* vault denies all structural logic; and why not, since structure, and its formal concomitants, is not its purpose. Its purpose is to produce the right kind of visual effect for the ceiling, and in those terms only must it be judged. Among gothic vaults it is nearest to the net-vault of German and Eastern European gothic (e.g. St Martin, Landshut). The principal roof spans 90 feet/27.43 metres, and is a concrete shell, 4 in/101.6 mm thick, with post-tensioned tie-beams. A cat-walk is set between this roof and the vault.

The Southern Screen Wall

Some accounts refer to the southern screen wall as the 'west window', using liturgical directions; certainly, English gothic cathedrals tended to have a wide screen-front, as the façade of the wall opposite the high altar. Some (e.g. Wells) have a big display of saints and kings. Here, we have the same, except that it is present inside as well as outside. The artist was John Hutton, originally from New Zealand, who had done similar work before on a smaller scale (pp. 112–13).

The figures depicted are as follows, (from the left, from inside, from top to bottom):

FIRST ROW (*first row of saints*): Angel, Isaiah, Elijah, David, Moses, Abraham, Angel.

SECOND ROW (*first row of angels*): Flying angels, St Michael, Flying angels.

THIRD ROW (*second row of saints*): St Paul, St James, St Peter, John the Baptist, Virgin Mary, St John, St Luke, St Mark, St Matthew.

FOURTH ROW (*second row of angels*): Flying angels

FIFTH ROW (*third row of saints*): St Aidan, St Oswald, St Augustine, St Columba, St Alban, St David, St Patrick, St Andrew, St George.

SIXTH ROW (*third row of angels*): Flying angels.

SEVENTH ROW (*fourth row of saints*): St Thomas à Beckett, St Osburg, St Alfred, St Margaret of Scotland, St Bede, St Hilda, St Chad, St Cuthbert.

EIGHTH ROW: Angel of the City of God, (*Door*), Angel of the Eternal Gospel, Angel of the Ascension, (*Door*), Angel of the Resurrection, Angel of Gethsemane, (*Door*) Angel of the Annunciation.

The subjects were originally to be saints only, but then angels were suggested. Bishop Gorton asked Hutton: 'Do you believe in angels?' 'Not really,' he answered; but he certainly *did* as a great help in designing the window. 'Quite right, so do I,' said the bishop. The 'window' is 70 feet/21.33 metres high, 45 feet/ 13.71 metres wide, and weighs 20 tons/20.32 tonnes. The panels are 8 feet/2.43 metres high and nearly 3 feet/0.914 metres wide. The screen's frame, of manganese bronze alloy, is hung from the roof, and stiffened by tie-rods (designed, like the other structures, by Ove Arup). There are ninety engraved panels and over fifty-two of plain glass. In their rows, the humans are placed in self-contained niches; the angels spread across from side to side, trumpets and wings being consciously used to pull the images across the wide mullions, producing a continuity of picture-space and composition. The humans tend towards the hieratic and two-dimensional; the angels (except the bottom row) lurch about, gaily, in a deep space (p. 167). Hutton first drew the figures on black paper, 2 feet/0.609 metres high, then they were enlarged photographically to full-size. They were engraved using a grinding wheel; the engraved face is inside. The artist has managed to produce considerable effects of illusory perspective, using low relief, as sculptors sometimes do, to give an effect of a fully-three-dimensional work: with a semi-profile (e.g. St Cuthbert) this effect of depth is very strong. The glass is only $\frac{3}{8}$ in/9.5 mm thick. In addition, Hutton produces the effect of semi-tones, as in a monochrome photograph broken into gradated dots for printing. The engravings have the same ambivalent nature as the whole glass screen: they appear light when seen against solid matter (the walls opposite) and dark when seen against the sky. As we move, and the background changes, they flicker in and out of 'positive' and 'negative'. Pevsner claims that Henry Moore's wartime drawings are the source for the graphic style:

The floor of the new cathedral, at its southern end, the light projecting figures from John Hutton's glass screen wall across the inscription of brass letters.

presumably he refers to the effect of the swathes of drapery-like substance, that swirls around Moore's people sheltering from the bombing, and Hutton's angels and saints.

Beneath, an inscription is set in the floor (43):

TO THE GLORY OF GOD +
THIS CATHEDRAL BURNT
NOVEMBER 14 AD
IS NOW REBUILT + 1962
(letters in brass, by Ralph Beyer, 3 feet/0.914 metres high)

Slightly beyond this, a maple leaf is similarly inlaid. Made in brass by Caroline Brown (2 feet/0.609 metres wide), it commemorates the money donated for the rebuilding by the people of Canada. Spence, Howard, and Clifford Ross undertook a gruelling fund-raising trip there in 1953. Beyond the maple leaf, a brass Chi-Rho is set. In the body of the nave (44) we see the chairs (design commissioned from R. D. Russell, made by Gordon Russell), and beside them the kneelers whose embroidered patterns depict fish, water, Chi-Rho, doves and a Tree of Life (see p. 115). From the middle of the nave, we perhaps get our most complete view of the great tapestry, *Christ in Glory in the Tetramorph* (45), designed by Graham Sutherland (below, see also pp. 114, 116).

The Tapestry

A statement of the tapestry's subject was written by R. T. Howard on 22 December 1951; it required depiction of 'Christ the Redeemer, in the glory of the Father, shedding his Spirit upon the Church'. Four specific elements were then described: 'the glory of the Father', 'Christ in the glory of the Father', 'the Holy Spirit and the Church' and 'the Heavenly Sphere'. Sutherland was directed to the *Revelation of St John the Divine*. Ch. 4, vs. 2, 3, 6 & 7 describe One sitting on a throne, surrounded by four living creatures. From the Early Christian period, these creatures had been associated with the four Evangelists, and similar creatures are found in the visions of Ezekiel. Sutherland spent a long time studying Christian art and iconography (particularly of the early centuries), and had a great liking for Egyptian sculpture. Because of the supreme importance of the central figure of Christ, he devoted years to a search for the right basic form for this figure, and then agonized long over the posture, gesture, physiognomy, vesture and overall effect of the Christ. He decided to produce a figure

One of the four beasts—the lion, associated with St Mark—from Revelation Chapter 4, a detail from Graham Sutherland's great tapestry.

possessed of divinity, of *mysterium tremendum*, having the stillness and tranquility of the Byzantine *Christ Pantocrator* image, and the 'quality of pent-up force' he found in the Valley of the Kings sculptures. He studied what we might call 'body language', and where the three cartoons differ most is in the positions of the arms and hands. The arms lowered and opened (first cartoon) most clearly approximate to the idea of Christ 'blessing, helping, ... drawing Humanity up into Himself', of Howard's statement. Their final position resulted from Sutherland's studies of actual gestures involved in religious activity, e.g. those of the Pope.

In the cartoons, the figure actually sits, but in the final work, the posture is somewhat ambiguous. Sutherland changed the drapery scheme when the work was on the loom; he did it to modify the rhythm of the drapery's forms, but he did not object to the ambiguity. A sitting figure can have far less 'presence' than a standing one, and the loss of stated perspective helped to create the blend of realism and conceptualism, in the figure, and the drapery, that the artist wanted. The absence of perspective is related to the hieratic, Byzantine-Romanesque qualities, productive of 'stillness'; but the lighting of the face

141

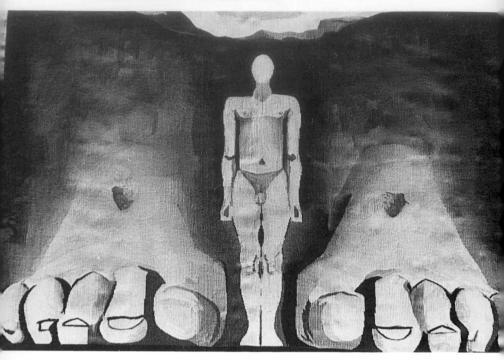

Detail from Graham Sutherland's great tapestry showing the feet of Christ, and a representation of a man—said to be life-size—between them.

(from a point above Christ's left shoulder) links the figure to the vestigial perspective of the illusory box, created by yellow lines above and behind Christ (this pictorial space jars against the real one, against the Lady Chapel's low-pitched concrete beams). Because of the figure's lack of depth (and other reasons) it is vital to see it through the 'tunnel' created by the Lady Chapel walls—reproductions fail that present only the actual tapestry in a frame. From another box-like space comes the 'light unapproachable', above Christ, that Howard's statement suggested as a permissible representation of the Father. In four squares, either side of Christ's mandorla, are the representations of the four creatures. Sutherland avoided all heraldic or stylized devices for these, considering that 'only through [the] demonstration of their nature do animals pay unconscious tribute to the power which created them'. He drew animals in zoos, trying to capture their real, beastly, qualities. He had most difficulty with the eagle, and considered various forms,

The head of Christ: detail from Graham Sutherland's tapestry Christ in Glory in the Tetramorph.

including a sphinx-like creature. The horizontal strips set either side of the creatures' 'boxes' derive from the funerary bands of Egyptian interment, and the placing of a man between Christ's feet (seen directly at eye-level) is of Egyptian origin also. The Devil is seen fleeing from Michael on Christ's left and may be symbolically present in the form of the serpent in the chalice.

The tapestry dominates the interior by its vast figure, and the strange personal *and* wholly-other qualities that Sutherland managed to give it. Thanks to the clear glass and white walls of the Lady Chapel, the powerful colour shines with the correct quality: not too flat, but not of the luminosity of glass (a product of the medium, surely). Time and again, people have found the lower part of the central figure odd; the swirling oval too easily suggests some insect's abdomen, and swells gravidially, almost before our eyes—but our eyes do not long stray from the gaze of Christ's.

The tapestry measures 74 feet/22.55 metres by 38 feet/11.58

metres. It consists of cotton warps and woollen weft. Australian and French wools were dyed to produce over 900 colours. The colours subtly reproduce the painterly qualities of the cartoon (enlarged photographically from a painting 79 in/ 2.007 m by 43 in/1.092 m) but reveal, as the use of photographic enlargement itself does, that the work was conceived in terms of painting and adapted to tapestry, rather than conceived as tapestry. The hanging of the tapestry down the length of the warp is unusual, as sagging can occur; this tapestry's long strips of crinkled textile have an odd seersucker-like effect (*The Lady Chapel* section, see p. 155.)

The Baptistery

From half-way between the baptistery and the Chapel of Unity, we get a good overall view of the former's stained glass window (22), though every viewpoint and proximity to it, adds something new. John Piper (born 1903), who designed the work, is an artist who has used very many media. A theme that runs through much of his work is architecture, as in his architectural photography (and architectural writings), and as a subject for much of his representational graphic work (a painting of the ruins of St Michael's is in the Herbert Art Gallery). Spence was impressed by Piper's windows for the chapel of Oundle School (1955–56). These are representational ('not realistic, but recognizable' (Pevsner)), but the architect wanted an abstract work for Coventry, principally because of the commanding presence of the figure of Christ in the tapestry (two such subjects would compete and clash), also, the depth of the stone mullions (at times they produce a chequerboard of dark stone against light glass) would be against a single figurative scheme or programme. There are 195 panels of glass. The window is 80 feet/24.38 metres high and 51 feet/ 15.54 metres across. Piper's cartoons (some are on display in the Visitor's Centre) were made into stained glass by Patrick Reyntiens, with whom Piper collaborated again shortly afterwards, producing the windows of the lantern of Liverpool Metropolitan Cathedral. The glass was installed between May and October 1961 (see also pp. 113, 116). The window has a great golden disc at its centre, composed of yellow and white glass: it has often been said that even on a dull day, it still shines. Beneath this are what Spence calls 'earthy' colours which 'reach up'—many greens and reds; above the sun-burst are 'celestial' colours—different shades of blue. The effect of

The font, showing the scallop-shaped bowl carved in it by Ralph Beyer.

the work at a distance is a grand, compelling unity, vast in size (bigger than Gloucester's east window) and very moving; but it, and the nave windows, raise the inevitable question of all abstract religious art, that of meaning. This work has no actual *meaning*—but at the same time is 'meaningful' by way of its beauty and grandeur. As we move towards it, we get a very different effect—we see the work in detail, each individual panel as it really is, and there see the very varied and richly-coloured compositions of forms. We can only see the lower parts thus, of course, and they are filled with squared and jagged shapes, and softer, tree-like forms.

The baptistery (46) is perhaps a misnomer, since the word properly implies some kind of chapel, transept, screened-off area, or separate building—a defined space. This is just a bulge in the perimeter wall (try to imagine the Piper window if the wall was straight), and there is no screen, or even a raised floor area. The font is a rock from a valley near Bethlehem, carved with a scallop-shaped bowl (p. 116). To Spence, this rock

One of the Tablets of the Word, carved in situ *by Ralph Beyer, and showing how simple depictions and devices accompany biblical text.*

represented the 'fundamental primitive feeling' he experienced in the caves of Lascaux (p. 98). Spence's original font and font-cover design (p. 106) was abandoned. When first used, the font was filled with water from the River Jordan. The attaching of special significance to this rock (and the water) because of its place of origin, whimsically perverts the true meaning and theology of baptism, reminding us of the special significance given to the sites of Jesus's life and death by the Emperor Constantine, who regarded them as specifically holy places. Suppose we discovered that the real Bethlehem boulder had been lost *en route*, and that what we have here is a replacement, secretly obtained by an embarrassed transportation company, from a Derbyshire hill-side: would we then continue to regard it in the same way? Would it matter?

The octagonal plinth, beneath the rock, is the only concession to the *true* iconography of baptism (from early times, fonts and baptisteries were hexagonal or octagonal, to suggest the days (6th and 8th) on which Jesus died and rose again, events with which baptismal candidates are symbolically identified in

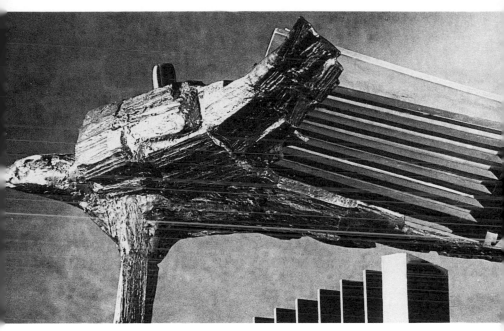

The eagle lectern, the work of Elisabeth Frink.

their ritual death and re-birth). Of course, the Bethlehem boulder is very evocative to many.

The East Nave Aisle

On the plain wall, to the left of the baptistery, we see the large crucifix carved in wood by Jindrich Severa (47). The figure is set into the wood, a low-relief in intaglio, hence, Christ seems to be bound into the cross's enveloping form. This, like various artworks, was added after Spence ceased to be involved with the cathedral.

Proceeding north, along the eastern nave aisle, we come to the first of the canted walls that make up the saw-tooth effect (see pp. 100–1); the walls' white finish strongly affects the interior's light and space. Set on it is one of Ralph Beyer's eight Tablets of the Word (48). Beyer's father had studied early Christian inscriptions, and seen how small symbols and devices had been incorporated into the lettering (p. 113). This idea was adopted here, the biblical texts being complimented with appropriate graphic element. *Whoso eateth my flesh and drinketh my blood hath eternal life* (the Tablet at the northern end of this aisle) is complimented with a simple depiction of chalice and host. From this aisle, we can look up to see the edge of the vault, from beside which large studio-lights can descend for the televizing of events: such lights were installed as a gift from the BBC, in 1962. Towards the end of the nave, we come to the sanctuary area (49) with its lectern (50), pulpit (51) choir-stalls (52), and beyond, to the left, the bishop's throne or *cathedra* (53). We can see that while there is no screen or *pulpitum*, the arrangement is liturgically traditional (for the evolution of the liturgical scheme, see pp. 92, 107). The two ambos indicate the normal cantoral and decanal duality. The lectern (50), instead of having the traditional brass eagle, has a bronze one, perching with wings outspread, by Elisabeth Frink (born 1930). Frink's subjects, particularly in the 1950s and 1960s, made much use of bird and animal forms, some being modelled in a very vigorous semi-abstract way—as this is. Critics have referred to her 'ferocious bronzes of birds . . . beaks out-thrust to stab at living flesh . . . ' (Robert Melville) and the 'grating edge and mute drama' of her early works (Sheldon Williams). The lectern and pulpit (51) are made of Afrormosia, and finished in bronze; they are very simple and must be among the dullest examples of ambo design.

The choir stalls are backed by something resembling a very long folding screen, and above them, in place of the oak tracery of the gothic cathedrals, there are canopies created by the multiplication of wooden 'triads', which form what Provost Williams called a 'thorn-like avenue'. Above the provost's stall is an object representing the flames of the Holy Spirit (Elisabeth Frink) (54). At the centre of the liturgical space, is the altar, of white concrete (55), and above it, the altar cross is seen, the work of Geoffrey Clarke (56). The cross's vigorous forms—so unlike those of the Chapel of the Cross's cross—enfold the original Cross of Nails (now silver-plated) Coventry's symbol of resurrection from the death of war's destruction. The altar is very long and large, but it needs to be, to stand against the overpowering tapestry. At the ends of each side-aisle we see the pipes of the organ, built, and restored, by Harrison of Durham. The configuration of the pipes are assymmetrical, but balanced.

OPPOSITE: The interior looking north (liturgical east), with the high altar and Lady Chapel beyond.

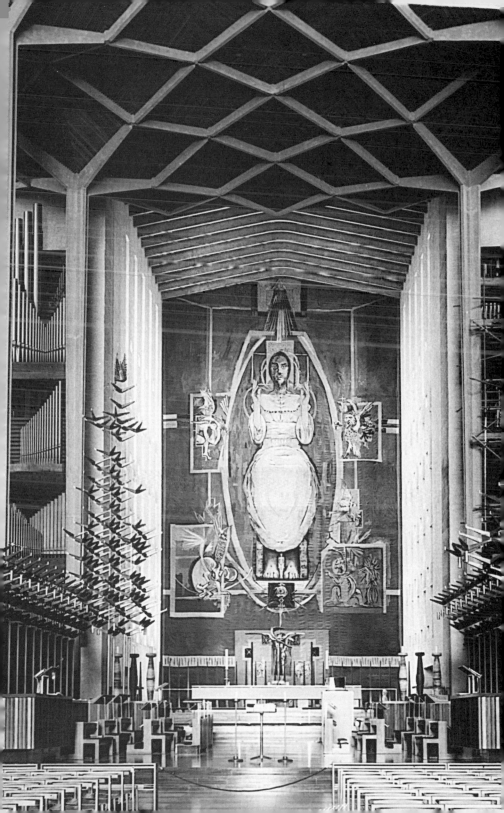

LEFT: *The high altar cross, with the Cross of Nails set within it. Beyond are the windows of the Lady Chapel's western wall, and below, the vertical members of the Lady Chapel's screen.*

RIGHT: *The western nave aisle, showing the arrangement of the organ pipes, the Tablets of the Word, the plain, rendered nave walls, and the back of the clergy-stalls.*

Early in the design process, Spence consulted Sir Ernest Bullock, an eminent organist, on the matter of music and acoustics. The choir (in the architectural sense) had to be planned in conjunction with the organ, and music facilities. There were many problems. Bullock advised moving the stalls closer together, but this would have counted against the visual impact of the altar. Bishop Gorton seems to have been somewhat against choirs, but determined, as Spence was, to have a prominent altar. Collaboration with the noted architectural acoustician Hope Bagenal broke down and, for all the effort put into these matters (p. 110), the liturgical acoustics are not deemed a success. The building is a superb setting, however, for large musical performances. As the building's completion moved near, the authorities commissioned Benjamin Britten, Arthur Bliss and Michael Tippett to compose special works, to be performed in a Coventry Cathedral festival. On 30 May 1962, Britten's *War Requiem* was performed in the cathedral, a choral setting of the Latin mass for the dead, interposed with settings for soli of the tragic war poetry of Wilfred Owen. The performance, in this poignant place, where the consequence of war was so vividly to view, must have produced an emotional effect of tremendous power upon those present. The music is suffused with sad evocations of destruction and death—the plangent tones of bells and gongs—and mournful moans of horns, as bugles calling men from 'sad shires'. The *Dies Irae* unleashes an overpowering drama, but its triumphant crescendi are riven with undertones of despair.

The Gethsemane Chapel

Continuing along the eastern aisle, the glinting gold of the Gethsemane Chapel's mosaic beckons us, as we pass more Tablets of the Word (Spence considered that this mosaic would be the first thing visible, on entering the building). On our right we see *The Plumb-line and the City*, by Clarke Fitz-Gerald (57), a sculpture involving a large metallic representation of a city with a vast builder's plumb-bob above it (added early 1970s). The Chapel of Christ in Gethsemane (58) is approached by ascending some shallow steps beneath the organ-pipes, and crossing a space that runs east–west, behind the altar. Spence designed a chapel that was something to look *into*, a little box with lighting carefully arranged, from a hidden, oblique, light-source, to fall on Steven Sykes's glowing mosaic of an angel, and the three —much less visible— sleeping apostles. The text is given as St Luke Ch. 22, v. 43–6, but the angel's cup probably makes reference to that in verse 42. The angel is understood as St Michael. Christ is not present in the work. The relief is made from *ciment fondu*. The Crown of Thorns grille (reminiscent of the bramble-motif that adorns the best late nineteenth-century illustrated books) has a big round hole, through which we cannot but peer in. Someone sitting in the chapel, facing the altar, must be conscious of being looked at. The chapel uses the best Baroque theatricality, Bernini could hardly have done better. His Cornaro Chapel presents a 'set', that we look *into*, but it does not turn us into what (being in Coventry) we must call Peeping Toms, to quite the same degree. Plans have been considered for rectifying this shortcoming.

The Chapel of Industry

Turning right, a narrowing passage takes us towards the light of the Chapel of Industry, otherwise the Chapel of Christ the Servant (59). The old guild chapels of St Michael's (pp. 45 ff.)

were originally to be replaced with a new Guild Chapel, and as such this cylindrical projection was designated and known, during the design and construction stages. It then became the centre of the cathedral's mission to industry, one of the features of the new approach to ministry that Coventry Cathedral devised. The floor is *c.*13 feet/3.96 metres above street-level. The laminated oak altar, 5 feet/1.52 metres square, stands in the centre above a circular stone plinth, in which are cut the words *I am among you as one who serves* (St Luke Ch. 22, v. 27). The ceramic candle-holders are by Hans Coper, and the aluminium cross (18 feet/5.48 metres tall) and jagged Crown of Thorns construction, are by Geoffrey Clarke. The ceiling is covered with gold leaf. Just inside the chapel, set in the floor, are the words: *If I your Lord and Master, have washed your feet Ye also ought to wash one another's feet* (St John Ch. 13, v. 14).

The Chapel of Industry is another very light space, with long panels of clear glass, between narrow concrete posts (see p. 100). Again, one receives the impression that the spaces of Coventry Cathedral were created for those who prefer (to use a transportation metaphor) the Alpine cable-car to the underground, or subway, train; yet Spence hoped that Coventry's medieval glass (pp. 70) could eventually be inserted here. It seems now that this may never happen, and perhaps a medievalized Chapel of Industry may not have been appropriate—though probably very beautiful. Often, the chapel is roped-off, and we find ourselves peering in, again.

Returning along the passage (it is easy to forget the steps, at this moment) we come to a circulation-spine that is the equivalent of the ambulatory passage that runs behind a gothic high altar. Here we discover that the altar cross (56) is free-standing, and set some way *behind* the altar on a plinth—not the way it looked before. The altar has two candlesticks fixed from behind, but to each side are three free-standing ceramic candlesticks, each said to be about the height of a person, and the largest 'thrown' pots ever made. They are the work of Hans Coper, and one of the last items installed before the 1962 consecration (60). The bishop's throne (53) is surmounted by a Christmas-tree-like canopy topped with a silver-gilt mitre (by Elisabeth Frink).

The Nave Windows

From this point we get a superb view of the nave's ten side-windows, and Spence intended that they should be seen from

Three of the six candle-holders, set beside the high altar (work of Hans Coper), each is about the heigh of a person.

the altar, possibly after receiving communion, and throw their light onto the altar (in earlier plans, the view of them, from here, was to have been through a reredos-screen: p. 107); and naturally, people look back at them as they proceed up the side-aisles. The work of Laurence Lee, Keith New and Geoffrey Clarke, of the Royal College of Art (p. 112), they are said to be the largest single stained glass commission ever. Spence's idea was that the nave windows represented (in pairs) the stages of the religious life, from birth to afterlife; and so they present a physical progression—from the baptistery to the high altar—analogous to the actual progression through life; as each stage is reached, the next is yet to be known (subsequent windows are hidden)—only when the last stage is reached, can all be known together. Further, Provost Williams described the symbolism as that of the quest for the truth about mankind, and about God, and the relationship between these two. These programmes and interpretations can be briefly described, from south to north:

FIRST PAIR (*greens*) Youth: (*a*): beginnings, creation, the emergence of life. (*b*): God's creation of the human race.

SECOND PAIR (*reds*) Early Adulthood (Spence: 'the age of passion'): (*c*): the emerging relationship of God and his people. (*d*): the response of people to God.

THIRD PAIR (*yellows; reds*) Middle Life (Spence: 'joys and sorrows, triumphs and disasters'): (*e*): the spiritual struggle. (*f*): the struggle with evil in the world.

FOURTH PAIR (*blues; purples*) Old Age (Spence: 'the richness of experience and wisdom'): (*g*): the flowering of life lived by faith in God. (*h*): Jesus's sufferings and saving acts—and the sacrament (cup of suffering/chalice).

FIFTH PAIR (*yellow; gold*) Afterlife: (*i*): human knowledge of the divine. (*j*): Jesus's resurrection, the Kingdom of Heaven and City of God.

The windows are 70 feet/21.33 metres high, and were installed by G. King & Son of Norwich. Different windows were produced by different artists: Lee: (*c*), (*d*), and (*i*); New: (*a*), (*b*), and (*e*); Clarke: (*f*), (*g*), and (*h*); (*j*) was the work of all three.

The canted windows are fundamental to Spence's design. It is a pity, *visually*, that we see them only with difficulty, since few stand at the altar for long, and the view from behind the altar is obstructed (try to imagine the saw-tooth reversed, and all windows visible in one, from the door!) but such considerations negate Spence's symbolic didacticism. The problem of such symbolism is the means of receiving understanding of it. When the windows were first exhibited, in London, opinions were canvassed, and a businessman said: 'I can't understand all the themes, but the colours are wonderful. They make one want to understand.' If an unscrupulous guide-book writer printed an entirely bogus programme, introducing totally different meanings, would the innocent reader/visitor realize it? Also, looking south, we see the tower of the City Hall, which, from beyond the ruins' walls, closes the southern axis.

LEFT: Sculpture of Our Lady, by John Bridgeman, in the Lady Chapel.
RIGHT: View into the Lady Chapel through the screen which forms its southern side.
The lower portion of the great tapestry— the crucifixion—forms its reredos.

The Lady Chapel

Behind us is the Lady Chapel (61), entered through a screen of vertical lance-like (or even oar-like) forms. The concrete altar has a strange horizontal slot in it. The chapel is rectangular or, rather, slightly trapezoidal, and provides what appears to be an awkward liturgical space, though it is used for many of the daily services. The lower portion of Sutherland's tapestry forms its reredos, or altarpiece. There were various projected schemes for this; some included Marian iconography (e.g. Pieta), but the final subject was a crucifixion. The chapel contained no reference to Mary in 1962, but now has the polyester-resin sculpture of *Our Lady* by John Bridgeman (62).

The tapestry's crucifixion presents a lifeless, even destroyed, Christ, his body hanging down with such a dead-weight as to bend, even crack, the 'horizontal' of the T-cross; the eyes seem too firmly closed ever to open again. The swirling forms flanking the figure represent the eclipsed sun and moon. The verticality and attenuation of this crucifixion contrasts with the strong horizontal element of the crucifixion at St Matthew's, Northampton (1946) with which this Coventry work must be compared. Both employ some vicious-looking thorns—a virtual

Sutherland *leitmotif,* particularly at this time. Again, many types of crucifixion were considered, some with forms more like the extant Northampton work, others with bodies even more stretched and emaciated, and some with a gothic curve in the body. Sutherland considered that the crucifixion involved 'the most tragic of all themes, yet inherent in it is the promise of salvation', and was the 'symbol of the precarious balanced moment [of good consequences or ill] . . .'. Here, observing the tapestry closely, we can see how the many colours of the woollen thread are blended to produce a whole.

The West Side of the Nave

Proceeding west, we come to an area that balances the Gethsemane chapel (here Spence originally planned to create a Children's Chapel). Opposite us are five stained glass windows designed by Einar Forseth (see pp. 115–16). Made in Sweden, they were transported to Coventry in sections (63). Subjects depicted include English missionaries who took Christianity to Sweden (St Sigfrid, St Bothvidh), emblems of the British nations, texts, and a dedication. Unfortunately, the tonality of the windows is totally out of balance with that of all the other stained glass works (which *do* have an overall harmony)—and this issue raises the important question of whether the cathedral, and its contents, has a unity or wholeness (see pp. 168 ff.). From here, we can descend to the basement, where the Visitor's Centre, Refectory and Gift Shop are situated. (See below, p. 158.)

Returning south along the western side-aisle, we see, set in the floor, some of the many coins, specially minted, and now worn, that act as markers for processional use (they show people where to stand), and each is a 1962 old penny (0.41666 p). The cathedral's marble floors are composed of stone from Kellymount (black), Hadene (cream-grey), and Darbydene, Derbyshire (mottled brown), all laid by Harry Edmonds, Marble Mason. We now see the nave windows close-to, and occasionally observe the slightly odd presence of human figures amongst the abstract and semi-abstract forms.

The Chapel of Unity

Finally, we come to the space that leads into the Chapel of Unity (33); this can be used as a stage. Inside it, in front of us, stands a sculpture of the *Head of the Crucified Christ* (64) by Helen Jennings (1969). A notice explains that it is made from

Interior of the Chapel of Unity, showing the variations of light quality produced by the sets of windows, the light revealing the textures of different materials: slate, render and concrete.

the metal of wrecked cars (not that it appears as such, like some junk-metal sculptures); it is presented as a comment on human destructiveness. The narrowing, transparent space leads us into the Chapel of Unity (32), dedicated 12 June 1962 (for its function and origin, see pp. 70, 83 ff.). It is a small cool space (it is air-conditioned). Its flange-like walls reach upward and seemingly inward, and the floor is slightly dished (why?). The thin, vertical strips of stained glass are by Margaret Traherne (pp. 114). In the centre there is a circular, glass-topped table (it must not be called an altar); the black cross above it represents mourning for the Church's divisions. After the early 1960s, an oval, wooden canopy, resembling a Welsh fisherman's coracle, was added to the chapel, and is suspended over the area to the west of the table. It is fitted with light-units, and no doubt acoustically aids the speaker. Einar Forseth's floor mosaic (detail opposite) is composed of over 100,000 pieces of marble, and is 40 feet/12.19 metres in diameter. It was assembled by J. Whitehead & Co of Kennington, London, assisted by Trota Descha, and its subjects represent the four evangelists, five continents, a dove, and other traditional Christian symbols; in all, it has an excessively fragmented look.

This chapel is a very pleasant enclosure of space, and is quite unlike that other round projection, the Chapel of Industry, which it balances. The clear slit-windows set beside the stained glass ones, are very narrow (but notice how, at the top, they turn a right-angle, and create, in pairs, a kind of T-shape), but they, with the wide diagonally-set walls, and projecting triangular spaces of the stellar-plan, succeed in relating the tent-like interior to the sculptural exterior. As we leave this conical confinement, to our left we sometimes see the multi-layered effect of reflections and images that the angled planes of glass compound: reflections of nearby 11 Priory Row, the baptistery window, and, through these, sight of the cathedral's interior, beyond. Then, directly opposite, we are stopped in our tracks by the shining glory of the baptistery window. As all is now seen, and the exit to our right, this may well be the last, lingering image.

The Visitor's Centre

The Visitor's Centre, housed in the cathedral basement, is an exhibition area, and also corresponds to the 'cathedral treasury' displays found elsewhere. Its contents must in some measure be regarded as impermanent, but an account can be given of the principal exhibits. As we descend from beside the Swedish windows (63), from a half-landing, a curious peep-hole gives us sight of a Cross of Nails, in another, larger, space. When we get there, we find Sutherland's final cartoon, or maquette, from which his tapestry was actually produced, and there are several of his sketches (some show versions of the body of Christ (Lady Chapel crucifixion))—155 other studies, and the two earlier cartoons, are in the Herbert Art Gallery. Full-size cartoons for the baptistery window include some for the vivid crimson panels, and there are two full-sized cartoons for the 'west window'. In the northern windows, seven panels saved

Asia—one of the representations of the continents found in the Chapel of Unity's floor mosaics, the work of Einar Forseth.

from St Michael's ancient glass (p. 70) are displayed; they include a Resurrection, and six angels. Here at last we see the whole of the processional Cross of Nails that we glimpsed from the stairs, and also the original Charred Cross (brought inside in 1978: the one outside must be a replica!), and a painting of the consecration service, from beyond the altar, by Terence Cuneo, an artist who specialized in painting ceremonies. In glass cases, there are some fine sixteenth- and seventeenth-century flagons, a 1535 Coverdale Bible, and illuminated copies of the consecration Petition and Sentence. Also encased is a beautiful 1904 cope, presented in 1951; it depicts the Lamb of God. A crosier, from Denmark, has a staff consisting of a narwhal's tusk (it was used at the consecration); Bishop Lisle Carr's pastoral staff (given 1946) unscrews into separate pieces. Perhaps the loveliest exhibit is the altar set of cross and candlesticks, in solid silver, which commemorates Provost Morton. It was made in 1936 by Omar Ramsden (1873–1939), a member of the Arts and Crafts movement, whose early work (with Alwyn Carr) resembles Archibald Knox's Art Nouveau designs. His later style, as we should expect, seems to have been more angular. Provost Howard pulled these items from the burning St Michael's and to him we must be eternally grateful. It is to be hoped that they and the cope are used, if only occasionally, in the setting of worship, rather than being permanently relegated to the condition of art-gallery *objets*, to be gawped at—pleasant though it is to see them close-to.

Nearby we see works of a different order, a set of holograms, based on sculptures of the *Stations of the Cross*, by Malcolm Woodward. They are holograms of the type where the visual image remains inside an illusory three-dimensional space. Photographs and texts link their religious meanings to humanitarian issues. The Visitor's Centre attempts, in various ways, to tell the story of Coventry Cathedral. There are interesting photographs and reproduced engravings of pre-1940 St Michael's. The exhibition also seeks to explain the cathedral's meaning and significance: many visitors are from the generation that had no experience of the war that caused its re-building.

Chapter Seven

EVALUATIONS AND RE-EVALUATIONS

In THE CATHEDRAL PRECINCTS of Coventry, time seems strangely conflated. Many modern industrial cities have ancient remains to view—especially on the Continent—but here there is a particularly curious mixture of time past contained in time present. We have the legendary past of St Osburg, the remote past of Godiva and the first bishops of Coventry and Lichfield, the 'early modern' period of the 'heyday' of St Michael's, the late-Victorian world that brought St Michael's restoration, and then elevation; and finally we have the post-war years. These last are surely the hardest of all to understand. They are recent, yet in reality as firmly in the past as, say, the twelfth-century Bishop de Lymesey. They still exist in many people's memories, yet time can cheat memory just as surely as documents, relics and chance survival, can cheat time; and time marches onwards like some ruthless despoiler.

When Guildford Cathedral was consecrated in May 1961, the builders of Coventry Cathedral, their work nearly done, must have felt their building to be something very different, something modern and contemporary. In April 1960, Peter Hammond had published *Liturgy and architecture*. Hammond's principal concern was with the architecturally-created centrality of sacramental worship, as a sharing of the eucharist liturgy in the midst of all. Buildings designed to serve this new liturgy of the people needed, above all, a centrally-placed altar. Also in 1960, architect Frederick Gibberd had been awarded first place in the competition, held in the previous year, for a new cathedral for the Roman Catholic Archdiocese of Liverpool: his building was completely circular, with the altar in the centre. In the same year, the Anglican church of St Paul, Bow Common, London, was completed; it was begun in 1956. Its architects, Maguire and Murray, became members of the New Churches Research Group who together produced *Towards a church architecture* (edited by Hammond), in 1962. These buildings and books attempted to embody and propagate the ideals of the Liturgical Movement, which is the name given to the new thinking about worship that arose as a result of experiments carried out before the war in the Roman Catholic church on the Continent (and the probable source of Eric Gill's advanced ideas (p. 83)). Also in 1962, the Institute for the Study of Worship and Religious Architecture was established in the University of Birmingham.

The new church architecture had arrived, and Coventry Cathedral was not part of it, a fact that came as no surprise to many. A new movement had emerged, and as it grew and developed, the effect was to make Coventry Cathedral even more archaic. Liverpool's Metropolitan (archiepiscopal) Cathedral was consecrated in 1967; at the same time, an architectural scheme was being developed for the completion of Liverpool's Anglican cathedral. It was a gothic design that matched the previous work (which had been growing since 1904), and it used virtually the same traditional gothic building methods and materials. During the years in which the design was being built, Clifton Cathedral was built in Bristol (1970–73). It was another product of the new Roman Catholic liturgy, that had gained official sanction at the Second Vatican council (1962–65); it was a work of modern architecture, and had exposed concrete and aggregate structures. By 1980, when Liverpool Anglican Cathedral was finally finished, the reaction against modern architecture had produced movements in favour of architectural conservation, and of traditionally-derived architecture. The Post-Modern age had begun. An exhibition in 1981, of the work of Edwin Lutyens (1869–1944), helped to establish and promote the acceptability of a new classically-derived architecture (in 1929, Lutyens had produced a design for Liverpool Metropolitan Cathedral, which was abandoned after the war; only the crypt was built, but in 1979 David Watkin claimed that it would have been the greatest church in the world). These various movements and reactions involved the re-valuing of historic, nineteenth-century, and traditionally-styled churches and church art. To those with this new set of architectural values, Coventry's cathedral was a building filled with objects of the most passé and tasteless kind imaginable—but in itself, it was of a form that was intelligible, and of high quality in its use of traditional materials. So beside Coventry's medieval churches there is a building very new (by comparison with them) which very rapidly became a thing of the past. The tower of St Michael's, and Holy Trinity Church, somehow feel less aged than the 'new' cathedral; yet somewhere, this time-bound building can seem to contain something that liberates it.

The 'liturgical criticism' of Coventry Cathedral, in the early 1960s, was that it totally failed as a setting for the corporate liturgy, as it was then conceived. We have seen that Bishop Gorton, Giles Scott, and Basil Spence all laboured to create a building with a forward, free-standing altar in Coventry, and that it nearly produced the first cathedral to embody the new ideas, but failed at the twelfth hour. Dr Gilbert Cope, of the Birmingham University Institute referred to, took this particular critical approach in a radio talk late in 1962. He pointed out that the narrow communion rail at the end of the rectangular building prevented large numbers of people receiving communion in a reasonable time, and totally excluded any symbolic gathering around the altar, in the sharing of eucharistic meal. The building was essentially a screen-less version of the medieval arrangement, derived from the ancient abbey church, where a monastic choir made functional sense; but in a modern cathedral it meant having a collection of singers and officiants who separated the altar from the people, and for no conceivable reason. Preferable would have been the ancient basilican arrangement (altar forward with clergy, etc., behind it, which Gorton and Spence had planned) if a rectangular plan had to be adopted; but best of all was a centrally-planned arrangement, as at the abbey church of St John, Collegeville, Minnesota. For Cope, the visual dominance of the tapestry prevented the altar from being the principal focus, and even an excessively large altar (which had been created) could not correct that fault. Above all, Cope considered that the church had not been thought of in terms of its *function*, which he took to be religious worship of a communal, sacramental, kind. For many of these alleged failings, Cope blamed Spence's clients, and the inadequacy of their competition conditions. Basil Minchin, in his 1963 review of *Phoenix at Coventry*, took a

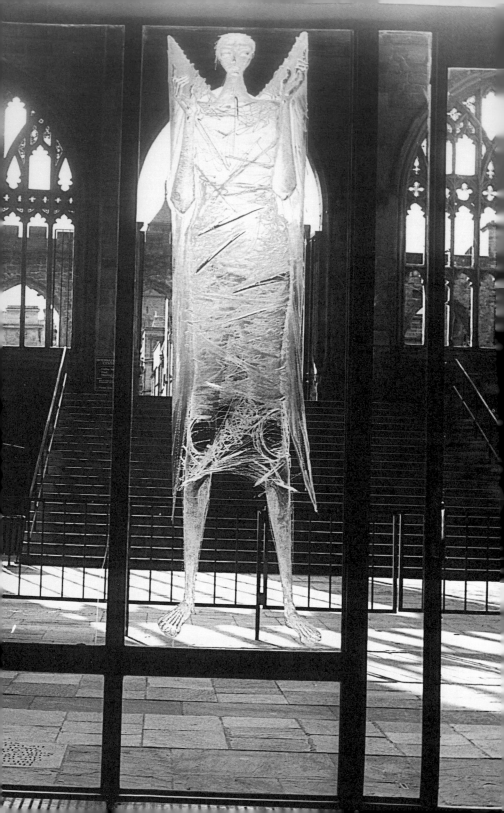

view similar to Cope's, complaining that the book constantly referred to 'what the building means and not enough of what is going to be done in it', and the conditions, he pointed out, defined function precisely in terms of the 'expression' of truths and religious 'witness'. Minchin questioned whether a church could have 'a valid meaning *apart* from that of the worship for which it was designed'.

Replying to Dr Cope's radio talk, in his talk of 29 November 1962, the Rev A. C. Bridge questioned the 'fashionable notion' that the eucharist (the *parish* communion, as it was known) was the 'supreme function of the worshipping Church'. Bridge wondered if this latest 'fashion in worship' would, in the evaluation of future generations, fare any better than those of previous centuries had, in the current view. Bridge then asked if a cathedral's function was 'solely or even primarily eucharistic?', preferring the view that it existed for large gatherings on special occasions, and its principal liturgy was that of the Word (preaching, teaching, etc.), not the Sacrament. Bridge then went on to defend the 'higher' functions of a cathedral, as a place to glorify God (in a validly Christian way) and as a place in which, and through which, 'all sorts and conditions of men' could glorify God. He also suggested that the centrally-planned building *could* symbolize an inward-looking Church, especially as the plan originated in the Byzantine period, whose theology involved detachment from the world.

Perhaps the most valid criticism of Cope's position, which Bridge seems to have been making, was that (on *this* occasion) he appears to have displayed a somewhat narrow view of religious architecture's *function*. The function, even the liturgical function, of a church, and particularly a cathedral, is clearly much wider than was suggested by Cope (and Minchin). Basil Minchin (and others since) have questioned the ability of such spaces as the Chapel of Unity and Chapel of Industry to function liturgically, as opposed to being symbols of religious ideals; yet it seems that they really are used as centres for their respective areas of mission, and long have been. Admittedly, the Chapel of Unity has had some modification. In looking, above, at the other chapels, questions were raised about their

OPPOSITE: Looking through the southern screen wall, showing an angel from the lowest row of engraved figures.

ability to serve as places for truly private worship and meditation. The crypt chapels are excellent for this purpose, except that they can not, in today's circumstances, be always open as places of easy resort. Many question such worship, and the validity of dark, quiet, private places of physical/spiritual retreat (some scorn 'individualist' religion), but to do so is surely totally to misunderstand religious faith, and Christian communality. We saw above how ideas for spaces and facilities, liturgical and otherwise, came and went—and some emerged and remained. The idea of a Christian Service Centre (anticipating, surely, some of the advanced ideas of the late-1960s and 70s) came early in Bishop Gorton's episcopacy. Two architects' designs for such a centre were approved; then, as building work proceeded, plans for the centre were reduced, and later, it was quietly turned into a refectory and gift shop (the present Visitor's Centre). A Chapel of the Resurrection was created in the ruins, planned for the new building, and then disappeared into the Chapel of Gethsemane. A Children's Chapel existed in the old cathedral, and was planned for the new. It was to have been sited near the present Swedish windows; then it 'moved' to the southern end, then was abandoned. The Chapel of Industry, as a concept, arrived at the last moment, out of the Guild Chapel; but the Chapel of Unity was conceived before the destruction, planned, built, and still exists.

The parish eucharist became, and will probably for some while remain, the central norm of Anglican worship; even those most disenchanted with the new liturgies, and their graceless language, would be unhappy in the deathly-dull matins-and-evensong world of the insipid Anglicanism of the 1920s, 30s and 40s, against which the 1960s' liturgists reacted. In consequence, the central altar is the norm, and unmoved Victorian eastern altars are almost as rare as the Georgian box-pews of St Mary, Whitby. Even in cathedrals there have been modifications and adjustments. In 1986, the Coventry Cathedral authorities considered various changes to the liturgical arrangements in the principal space, but nothing was implemented.

The new church architecture movement, in the mid- to late-1960s, evolved the theory of the multi-purpose place of worship. J. G. Davies, Director of the Birmingham Institute, attacked the idea of a church building being thought of as a specifically holy place, and originated the idea of the church as

Looking through the southern screen wall to the ruins.

a secular place, where all kinds of acts of worship and service to the community, could—and should—go on in the same space. Unlike in Chapters 1 and 3, 'secular' now means buildings, places and people, which are to be considered as neither ritually holy, nor profane; 'secular' is a neutral term, rejecting traditional dualism, and the concept of holiness found in Rudolf Otto's *Das Heilige*. Davies's *Secular use of church buildings* (1968) looked to the non-religious uses to which churches had been put in the past (pp. 59–60) and connected these with his defence of the multi-purpose church centre. This understanding of a church building involved (among other things) considerable flexibility of use. Coventry Cathedral had often been the scene of experimental worship and artistic events (the competition required facilities for 'liturgical movement'), things that went far beyond the bounds of traditional cathedral activities, and it was surely the pioneer, in this country at least, in the use of a cathedral for secular as well as sacred activities. The cover photograph of Davies's book shows a trio of female dancers, two gracefully entwined, the third, her bottom bulging from fish-net tights, looks on. Behind, two choristers stand, bemused, and from above, the piercing eyes of Graham Sutherland's Christ look quizzically down. Coventry's cathedral authorities were not pleased by the photograph's prominent publication, but at a glance it reveals something of what the cathedral 'was about' at the time—1967—(words must suffice—the photograph now seems unobtainable). The new building was *not* designed to be totally flexible for 'multipurpose' use (the chairs are movable, but the clergy stalls, ambos, and altar are not); yet Coventry has filled its walls (roofed and otherwise) with artistic, dramatic and musical events of all kinds, at the same time as developing its ministries to industry and of reconciliation (as with the international Community of the Cross of Nails—see W. E. Rose, *Sent from Coventry*, Oswald Wolff, 1980).

Spence designed a building to act as a setting for modern religious artworks, a 'casket' filled with 'jewels' (p. 112). They were, from the first, to be different works from different artists, in different media (this is the source of the old criticism that the church was a 'twentieth-century religious art gallery', or a 'religious Festival of Britain'). He went to leading artists of the day, and got them to produce individual creations which, he must have known, would stand proud as the products of a known artistic figure. In the time of, say, Truro Cathedral, and with gothic design and construction, all decoration, embellishment and even monuments, were part of the architect's overall design and all built up as an integral part of the basic fabric, the work being done by stone-carvers on site and stone-carving sculptors. With the Byzantine style this was not the same, so that Westminster Cathedral was built, then left for mosaicists to adorn and finish (or not finish, as was actually the case). At Liverpool, Scott continued the gothic tradition, and works of glass and sculpture were carefully integrated and subordinated to the whole. He did not commission (intentionally?) big names or any artistic *prima donnas*, and he even resorted to designing sculpture himself, in order to get the right effect. The result is unity, harmony, and integrity, the triumph of architecture—space and volume—over all else. Spence chose a different, more difficult, path. The filling of churches and cathedrals with works of modern artists 'of reputation' was the passion of Walter Hussey, first as vicar of St Matthew, Northampton (1937–55) and then as Dean of Chichester (1955–77), but this approach to cathedral building

was actually begun, I fancy, in the surprising setting of
Guildford Cathedral. Maufe's vast brick and rendered surfaces
are punctuated with stone carvings (e.g. Eric Gill's), which
appear to be stuck on as an afterthought, and there are various
other kinds of artwork addition (and Guildford has moments
of Coventry-like whimsy: the crosiers as door-handles). The
link with Coventry comes in the form of John Hutton and his
engraved-glass doors. (Of course Truro and Liverpool have
sculptures attached to the sides, but there they blend in as part
of the whole.) Spence's approach involved a much larger
vision, of his own; the very density of the inclusion of separate
artworks raises the questions of harmony and unity.

I am conscious that such things are in great measure
subjective. Many visitors do feel that everything 'goes
together', and others do not; on any day in the cathedral one
can easily discover members of either camp; but certainly we
can attempt to frame some understanding of the kinds of unity
that such a work might achieve, including those of overall
style, and of a common symbolic theme. Harmony of form is
rarely possible. Perhaps having several principal artworks is
preferable to having one major feature, thus producing a stool
standing on several legs. How many legs does it have? The
works upon which the whole rests are the tapestry, the
baptistery window, St Michael and the Devil, and the
engraved glass 'west window'. The last of these, however, is of
less total success than the others, for the whole concept of the
glass wall is one that surely few would consider a success, and
would wish to repeat.

The big name approach to religious art is very much that of
the Modern Movement, which praises artists for their indi-
vidualism, personal vision, and resolute refusal to indulge in
'compromise'. The modern or *avant garde* artist is really a post-
Romantic artist, one who sees art as personal expression, based
on private inspiration, and hence, the art exists—to a greater or
lesser degree—as a means of satisfying personal needs of one
kind or another. In the fifteenth century, an artist would create
exactly what was asked for and paid for, right down to the
smallest details (with Italian altarpieces, for example, the size of
blue areas as opposed to brown, would be dictated by the
contractual arrangements: the payment would take account of
the varying cost of different pigments). This kind of religious
art, like the church music of the day, was functional and the
artist simply produced what the patron commissioned and

what was actually needed in the situation in question. It would be inconceivable for a fifteenth-century artist to say 'this is my vision of St Michael, and I won't compromise!': such an artist would starve. Today, the absence of names leads us to see such people as the carver of St Michaels' misericords as some kind impersonal instrument of the forces that created the building. He would have been an individual artist, but his work would have formed part of the whole, and people would not have come from far and wide just to see *his* work (as they do to see Sutherland's and Epstein's), and a new commission at St Michael's, Coventry, would not have pushed up the price of his works on the London art market. The worst excesses of the big name artist approach were avoided at Coventry, probably by the careful planning of subject programmes by Provost Howard, etc., and the attention Spence, the bishops, and others, gave to supervising the commissions. For once, it seems, the committee approach worked.

When the Stations of the Cross were installed in the Visitor's Centre (p. 158), it was considered that if presented as holograms (which they were) more people would look at them, and read their message, than if they had been displayed as sculptures (which they could have been). So here, the criterion for religious art was the ability to easily communicate meaning. By this criterion, the baptistery window must be seen as a failure, because it communicates no meaning ('utter, informationless abstraction' according to Martin Pawley), or at least, not in the literal way that the hologram Stations of the Cross, with their accompanying images and words, do. But can the holograms be spoken of as artworks comparable with the baptistery window?—I doubt it. Meaning in religious architecture and art is a complex problem. We saw that the ruined St Michael's communicated something to people (p. 76) in a way that no contrived work of art or architecture probably could (and by 'contrived', I mean simply 'intentionally created for a particular result'). We saw that theologically, and in terms of Christian symbolism, the font is something of a travesty: and yet it is supremely meaningful to people who may not know, or care, about rituals of death and re-birth. The question of the religious nature or value of abstract art is one raised by the baptistery window, and the nave windows. Surely art can only be religious art if it can clearly and unequivocally express ideas that are specifically religious (in his 1984 book, Michael Day refers to church artworks' 'primary purpose of turning minds

The damaged remains of a nineteenth-century monument on the wall of the northern nave aisle of St Michael's.

and imagination towards God'). Some abstract works can have symbolism (e.g. baptisteries, p. 146), or rationally-created programmes (the nave windows), that are meaningful on elucidation or initiation. It may be argued that some (e.g. the baptistery window) may partake of the higher experience of the spirit, beyond rational experience, where truth can, with validity, be linked with beauty; but such a window as Piper's could arguably be installed in some large and suitable public building, of a non-religious nature, and there be just as 'meaningful', and in terms of other kinds of values.

Coventry Cathedral's 'jewels' have, like the building itself, been subjected to the test of time, and some have become dated more quickly than others. Some are real period-pieces, and can only speak of the late-1950s; others have broken away from such bonds, and it is interesting to note which these are. In 1962, as with the building, the contents must have looked frightfully modern; but, along with the architecture (but perhaps less obviously so) much of it was *not* the real thing. In the late 1950s, *avant garde* painting meant the paint-splashes of Pollock, not the work of Graham Sutherland, and the representational sculpture of Epstein was thoroughly *retardataire*. And these 'compromised' works are just those that seem to retain their power for most visitors. With art, as with architecture, the pendulum of taste swings on. The studies of Arts and Crafts movement sculpture, of such as Susan Beattie, have opened people's eyes to the extent that the kind of sculpture represented at Coventry by the Yeatman–Biggs memorial (pp. 42, 124) is at least as interesting as that represented by, say, Frink's eagle, though no previous book on Coventry Cathedral seems to have even mentioned Thorneycroft's effigy, a fault I have tried to correct (the Yeatman–Biggs memorial is not specifically a work of religious art, however).

Spence's design pleased neither the radical-moderns (liturgical and architectural) nor the ultra-traditionalists (who wrongly described it as a *concrete* monstrosity); but it pleased the assessors, and it pleased the Reconstruction Committee. The assessors were arguably an odd collection. Maufe undoubtedly had great experience of religious architecture, and knowledge extending beyond the confines of his own restrained gothic; yet the architect he was involved in effectively choosing was not (at this time) a church architect. Thomas and Robertson really seem to have had little to offer to this kind of project and situation. The cathedral authorities, it has been suggested, framed their requirements in a vague and inadequate way; and they surely had a poor architectural (as well as liturgical) understanding of what they wanted, and how it could be acquired. Some of Spence's first design-work for the cathedral (as seen in the competition detail-drawings, published in *Architectural Design*, September 1951) has a definite traditional feel to it, having the kind of historically derived intricate decoration found in the thoroughly conservative *Post-war church building* (Ernest Short, ed., 1948), and it must have looked odd beside the Festival of Britain work he had been producing at about the same time.

What are the sources of the building Spence produced? Pevsner saw its origins in the kind of church built by N. F. Cachemaille-Day (e.g. St Saviour, Eltham, London (1932–33); St Luke, Holbrooks, Coventry (1939) and St Barnabas, Tuffley, Gloucester (1939)). Cachemaille-Day's churches are original and unmistakeable. Many have a long, narrow rectangular volume, with high walls and long slit-windows. Externally, the sides are subdivided by vertical strips of brickwork, projecting diagonally outwards, and some, beneath their concrete roofs, have vestigial gothic-like rib-work. Vigorous brickwork of this kind derives from Dutch and Scandinavian work of the 1920s. They are authentically the product of the 1930s, yet not Art Deco, like the churches of F. X. Verlade. A cathedral-sized Cachemaille-Day church would have much in common with Spence's design. Spence's walls do seem to owe something to the Continental 1920s expressionist brickwork. The Coventry stonework, as has been suggested, recalls the architecture of the Arts and Crafts movement, and the northern façade (with its buttresses like gigantic versions of Voysey's, and its diagonal mullions reminiscent of the work of Randall Wells) seems to show more than an influence related to materials and their use. While Bishop Gorton certainly did not get the exciting Modernism at the cathedral that he seems to have wanted, Spence's design for a standard church and hall, to be duplicated, with variations, in different Coventry suburbs, was more thoroughly modern. They were built at Tile Hill (1957–58), Bell Green (1958) and Willenhall (1955–57). These were indeed the concrete box some observers of the cathedral competition had feared, each with the spindly concrete-frame tower, which so resembles the tower beside fire stations, whose function seems to be something to do with hoses, but with churches (many designers used them) is uncertain. At Willenhall, Spence used the 'western' glass screen wall, as at the cathedral. Spence's St Matthew, Reading (complete 1967) shows he quickly adapted to the Liturgical Movement approach to Anglican church planning (this, and the Coventry churches, were built to and required low budgets). The larger chapel of Spence's Mortonhall Crematorium, Edinburgh (also complete in 1967) shows a later use of strips of glass providing directional light onto the liturgical focus; but here, Spence seems to have total *control* of the light.

Various estimates of Spence as an architect, and ideas about his work, have been given above. Writers have pointed to the romantic and evangelistic nature of his personality and his art. His architectural tastes, listed in *Phoenix at Coventry*, are very varied and very revealing. He admired Corbusier, and also Gaudi, Spanish gothic, the Byzantine of Ravenna, and much else. In seeing him, as many have, as an architect determined, above all, to realize his personal vision, he has emerged as a designer for whom rational planning was subordinate.

Certainly, he was not a Functionalist, in the true Modern Movement sense (he was not a member of the MARS group). And yet while his Corb was the Corb of Ronchamp chapel (a 'manifesto of irrationalism' (Pevsner)) rather than of the *Unité d'Habitation*, he could create concrete tower-blocks along with other modern architects (e.g. the 1960s Gorbals high-rise housing, Glasgow). Clearly, Spence quickly moved on, as revealed in a 1965 radio interview, in which he confessed to being very critical of the cathedral design. Edward Mills sees some of the tower-block work (e.g. the Knightsbridge Barracks, 1977) as thoroughly Spence in its creation of a monumentality, which, while produced by modern means, ultimately derives from the influence of Lutyens. Spence's capacity for whimsy is seen in his surrounding of the Rome Embassy Chancery with water (to mark it out as an island, like Britain): in a lecture given to Southampton University, in 1973, he actually calls it a 'romantic idea'.

The innocent suggestion of the Coventry city council (around 1951) that the cathedral wait ten years before building, tantalizes us with questions of what would have *then* been built, by Spence, or any other. Certainly, there would have been a free-standing altar, and probably a *totally* modern style. How would such a building have fared? We could speculate as to how various *avant garde* entries to the competition would look, and work, today. I, and others, have criticized the effects produced by the glass screen wall: but the Smithsons' scheme seems to have involved even more glass, and more, bleaching, light. When we consider the problems relating to the building that have been experienced at Liverpool Metropolitan Cathedral, we might reflect on the possible consequences of some of the other entries, if built: only as Spence's cathedral approached its twenty-fifth year did attention to the stonework become important.

One desire of most post-1945 church builders was for a modern style of church building. 'It is essential that today the Church builder seeks to be contemporary. We need to build in the idiom of our time . . . Our buildings have to be examples of modern architecture, just as much as the blocks of flats or the shopping centres which may be near them . . .' This comes from *A Methodist church builder's decalogue* (W. Oliver Phillipson, 1966), but it could be from any other church-building book of the time, produced by any Christian denomination. Peter Hammond's *Liturgy and architecture* writes, at length, in this vein. Being contemporary, of our time, and 'speaking to the world in the language of the living', etc., these ideas became raised to the status of dogma. Involved here was a genuine and thoroughly understandable boredom with the centuries of historical architecture, which, in the austere 1940s and 50s could produce some very dull work. Three generations or more of Gothic Revival inevitably produced two which reacted, and were tired with the past. But now we are beyond that reaction and can see its ideas clearly. We can see a good measure of (real) Romanticism in such as Hammond's Ruskinian moralism (a traditionally-styled church would corrupt the taste *and faith* of its users, Ruskin saw the architecture that he disliked as corrupt and corrupting in every conceivable way), and also in the belief in the 'Spirit of the Age' (p. 93). Articles concerned with Coventry Cathedral by J. M. Richards and R. Furneaux Jordan (and Pevsner's 1951 article) all see the building or proposed building, in terms of its success or failure to be authentically 'of our age'. The architectural thinkers were gripped by 'belief' in a new architecture, it became a kind of pseudo-religion; the churchmen were gripped by the illusions of contemporaneity, and the enthusiasms of 'trendyism', by which I mean doing things for their own sake, and purely because they are thought of as 'of our time'; Giles Scott once wisely spoke of the 'morbid craving for originality *at any price*', and the price in question must always be integrity and the possibility of truth. 'Contemporaneity'—or whatever we must call it—*is* an illusion. In reality, buildings date from a real time, which is quickly in the past, since the present is always moving; but 'our time' is no *real* time at all. In fact, such writers were simply producing an elaborate justification—with all the casuistical skills with which their theological colleges had endowed them—for the kind of architecture their inclinations led them to. People who liked putting modern art in old churches had an argument that runs as follows: in each former century, wise old builders used their own styles and forms when they added their own to earlier work (with the resultant mixture of styles, etc., in old cathedrals). They did this because they believed in 'truth to our time'; so it is true to the past, and to *our* times, to make additions in concrete and fibre-glass today. In fact, of course, these earlier builders made their incongruous additions, destroying harmony and unity, because they knew no better, craftsmen being trained into one manner of work only; *really* wise, and sensitive, artists did *not* use their own styles, etc.: when completing Westminster Abbey in 1375, Henry Yevele used the style of the existing thirteenth-century work, and so created a harmonious whole. Modern people often have a taste for the mixtures of styles, etc., in old churches, and a tremendous respect for disordered medieval fragments and ruins: but these are the legacy of the Picturesque and Romantic movements of the late eighteenth and early nineteenth centuries, and such tastes were totally absent before then, and certainly in the Middle Ages.

And so we come to attitudes to old buildings and ruins, and the relation of new buildings to them. For all their ills, the nineteenth-century restorers had a practical and even realistic attitude to medieval remains. William Morris, however, saw gothic work as sacrosanct, and not to be restored, or even touched, preferring churches to collapse rather than be worked on by Sir Gilbert Scott; if this late nineteenth-century attitude had prevailed, and J. O. Scott's work had been prevented, we would have lost St Michael's wonderful tower for all time. Something of this reverence for medieval building is found in the thinking of such Modern Movement advocates as Richards and Jordan, in their Coventry articles. They see medieval cathedrals as *the* great works of religious architecture—but quite impossible to repeat, since in our time, the *zeitgeist* does not allow of it. Basil Spence took some of this thinking on board. His argument is that being part of tradition (of which he is respectful) is being modern, since the architects of the past thought purely in terms of the ideas of 'their own era'; so he was modern in order to be traditional, and traditional in order to be modern. His attitude to the ruins seems to be in the Morris tradition, and so for him there was to be no adding new bits to it here and removing bits there. He *might* have agreed with Laurence Whistler that the best architecture does not harmonize with old work that surrounds it, or with Robert Lutyens, that twentieth-century gothic is fake (p. 93), but he seems—by his lack of an *avant garde* approach, in his cathedral design—to have seen through the blind belief in contempora-neity, and had much greater vision, seeing that something utterly and totally of this moment, would, like the clothes of the day, be very quickly gone and forgotten (though some of the cathedral's contents, I have suggested, suffered just this fate). Spence produced a compromise, in his architecture, and its virtue was that by this means alone did he build something that could continue, long after the heady swinging Sixties, to

Ecce Homo (1934–5), Jacob Epsein's interpretation of Christ before Pilate, brought to Coventry in recent years.

be valuable and meaningful. The 'of our time' people held that things that were truly products of contemporary society would last, and stand the test of time (i.e., they thought that what *they* valued would always be valued), but I think that the opposite is the case: because Spence's building failed to be truly of its time (in the *avant garde* sense) it has succeeded in being able to be of other times also, and so Edward Mills is able to write: 'Time alone will decide the place of Coventry Cathedral in the history of British architecture.'

If the particular circumstances of Basil Spence's training, personality, and ideas, enabled him to rise above the cruder notions of his day (as I have suggested), how would he react today, in this Post Modern age, when we are all liberated from *zeitgeistism*, and the idea of styles created from processes of history? Now, architecture is just architecture, and each work is seen to succeed or fail in architectural terms (for a church, by way of its ability to fulfil its functions (liturgical, practical, symbolic, theological, etc.)), and the visual appearance is not the source of evaluations. Different styles are just different languages (p. 93), they are not pieces of ideology. The latest work at St Edmundsbury Cathedral (gothic, finished 1970) seems to shout this liberation. Ironically, modern-style architecture is the first to be liberated: it can now succeed in real terms, it can walk on its own feet, without the crutch of cranky ideas. People know that the only real spirits are in bottles, and that any style can be established as *the* necessary style of the age, if its backers have the best propaganda (Pugin knew this). A modern style is now seen as not having a *necessary* connection with functional success and flexibility: Edward Patey, on leaving Coventry to become Dean of Liverpool in 1964, showed that a traditionally-styled and planned building could be as adaptable and useable, for all kinds of events, as any modern-styled cathedral, and much more than some.

I seem to have suggested that the real value and merit of a major work of Christian architecture or art lies in its ability, by some means, to transcend its moment of making. No sensible artist would aim for eternity, as that would ensure failure, but the same result, I have claimed, comes from the preoccupation with the present. The Christian religion is one created out of historical reality—people and events in real time—but professes a hold on eternal truths that, of necessity, must transcend the temporal situation in which its message and mission are created and re-created anew. I said at the outset that a cathedral was simply the setting of a bishop's seat; this is true, but not in fullest truth. A Christian cathedral must be much more, more than a place that fully and successfully serves the liturgy— vitally necessary though that is—more, even, than the heart of a diocese or centre of a large community. I well remember, in the early 1960s, hearing of people who went to Coventry, not just to see its new cathedral, but equally, to see its super new shopping precincts—definitely a glimpse of the future! But now every town has its shopping precincts, and no one would cross the street to see one: but the same cannot be true of a cathedral, and is not, of this one. A cathedral is more than a shopping centre, and while it must function as well, its functions are more, and greater. More than ever before do we need built symbols of faith, things that serve as a centre of aspiration, creating some special locus of meaning. Such things reach, far beyond classic, historic, Christian symbols and signs, to some understanding at the extremity of ideas. This meaning is not other than the meaning of worship, but greater than the physical actualities of worship.

For all its liturgical failing, Basil Spence created something original, unique, and valuable, in his embodiment of destruction and resurrection; and out of the depths of his compromise and 'romantic visions' stirred up an interest and response that twenty-five years has not taken away. The success of the cathedral clearly perplexed those who appear to have been writing from a position totally outside of religious faith—so R. F. Jordan sees it as a failure, while acknowledging its capacity to inspire people in a religious way—as though it could have any other function. In purely architectural terms, there are many churches superior to this one, many more whole and coherent; but no other has this special combination of religious truth and physical object. Pevsner suggested that it was this singular, original idea that convinced assessors and committees, even if, as others have suggested, Spence's vision blinded them to practicalities. This architectural image can acquire the perpetual relevance of the Christian doctrine of resurrection it 'stands for': but this needs explication, since soon the generation that knew the war will be gone, and then, that which learnt of its horrors direct, from their parents. The response to this need, in recent times, has been an audio visual production, shown to visitors in the former Chapter House, telling the story of the cathedral's destruction and re-creation, and of its religious messages of resurrection and reconciliation. But naturally, such productions impinge upon the building itself (recorded air-raid sirens, and Vera Lynn, audible in the Chapel of Industry), and the line between medium and message is blurred. Yet without something, ruins and rebuildings could one day be unintelligible and strange, the former like some demolition-site whose workers are permanently on strike (in 1971, H. Gordon Slade saw the Charred Cross as looking like 'so much uncleared debris').

Recent re-evaluations have queried such matters. Martin Pawley's 1984 'Building Revisit' hammered the cathedral for its remorseless selling of *itself*, and of its myth; yet without myth there is little message. Soft-targets for this writer's criticism were the tasteless posters, set on the Visitor's Centre stairs, that reported rave reviews, not of the building (itself a medium for a message, and one that must be distinguished from its truth) but of the video show. Pawley also criticized the architecture, particularly the glass screen-wall (he tells us that Spence spent so long peering through his model's screen-wall that he failed to consider what it would be like to be inside; and indeed, we have noted a certain voyeuristic theme running through Coventry Cathedral, a legacy, no doubt, of the architect's intense exhibition design-work).

The old objectives and missions—purposes inherent in the 1962 foundation—have gone (reconciliation with Second World War enemies is accomplished), but now there are new needs and new purposes. Division and strife is different, but no less intense, in the world of Coventry Cathedral's maturing, and needs are not only in foreign places, but on the doorstep. The chasm between rich and poor, the gap between races and cultures, and all the problems of modern society, as we slide down the plummeting incline of the graph from that 60s high, these are the matters to which the cathedral would address itself. Perhaps the building can help with these new missions, perhaps it can inspire and serve in ways unintended and inconceivable to its creators. It is, after all, a platform, a stage, a forum (its architecture has made it so, so *open* is it), a place of meeting it is, and the bustle of activity, and of constant visitors, to whom there might be Christian communication.

And how will it be when its age has advanced much more? Will time's ever-rolling stream wash away the building's less beautiful contents—or will some future generation cherish them, as we do the work of earlier times? Will its physical reality provide an intelligible whole, when its original cultural context has all vanished? And will some new framework of Christian ideas and faith, our own gone, re-cast its images for its message?

The arms of Coventry's (modern) see, as depicted in the early diocesan calendars. It consists of: *Gules a Cross potent quadrat in the centre argent. A border of the last charged with eight torteaux.*

BISHOPS OF THE DIOCESE OF COVENTRY

H. W. Yeatman-Biggs, 1918–1922
C. Lisle Carr, 1922–1930
Mervyn G. Haigh, 1931–1942
Neville Vincent Gorton, 1943–1955
Cuthbert K. N. Bardsley, 1956–1976
John Gibbs, 1976–1985
Simon Barrington-Ward, 1985–

PROVOSTS AND TITULAR-PROVOSTS OF COVENTRY CATHEDRAL

C. E. Morton, Sub-Dean: 1929–1931; Titular-Provost: 1931–1933
Richard Thomas Howard, Titular-Provost: 1933–1937; Provost: 1937–1958
Harold C. N. Williams, 1958–1982
Colin Douglas Semper, 1982–

BIBLIOGRAPHY

PRINCIPAL SOURCES — BOOKS & MANUSCRIPTS

Alfred J. Brookes, **The bishopric of Coventry, the collegiate church of St Michael,** ND (**c.** 1910); **St Michael's church, past and present,** ND (**c.** 1906).

Roy Coad, **Laing,** Hodder & Stoughton, 1979.

A history of Warwickshire, v. 3 (City of Coventry and Borough of Warwick), University of London, 1969 (Victoria Histories of the Counties of England (VCH)).

R. T. Howard, **Ruined and rebuilt. The story of Coventry Cathedral, 1939–1962,** Coventry Cathedral Council, 1962.

Christopher J. Pickford, **The steeple, bells and ringers of St Michael's church, Coventry** (draft, 1986, of detailed study in preparation).

Andrew Revai, ed., **Christ in glory in the tetramorph. The genesis of the great tapestry,** Pallas Gallery/Zwemmer, 1964.

Royal Fine Art Commission, Committee Minutes, 1947, 1951 (Public Record Office).

Giles Gilbert Scott; Manuscripts, papers, etc., RIBA.

Basil Spence, **Phoenix at Coventry. The building of a cathedral,** Bles, 1962; Fontana, 1964.

N. T. Thurston, **Account of the re-building of Coventry Cathedral** (typescript in four folders, Coventry Cathedral, ND).

The west window of Coventry Cathedral (John Hutton, Robert Payne), ND, (**c.** 1962).

H. C. N. Williams, **Cathedral reborn,** English Counties Periodicals, ND (**c.** 1964). **A guide to Coventry Cathedral and its ministry,** Hodder & Stoughton, 1966; **The pictorial guide to Coventry Cathedral,** Pitkin Pictorials, 1967, etc.

Frederic W. Woodhouse, **The churches of Coventry,** George Bell, 1909.

ADDITIONAL SOURCES, BACKGROUND INFORMATION, Etc.

Lucy Archer, **Raymond Erith, architect,** Cygnet Press, 1985.

William Beresford, **Lichfield** (Diocesan Histories), ND, (**c.** 1880).

F. Bliss Burbidge, **Old Coventry and Lady Godiva,** ND.

Martin S. Briggs, **Goths and vandals,** Constable, 1952.

Angus Calder, **The people's war. Britain 1939–45,** Jonathan Cape, 1962.

Owen Chadwick, **The Victorian church,** Part 1, A & C Black, 3rd. ed., 1971.

Alec Clifton-Taylor, **The pattern of English building,** Faber, 2nd. ed., 1972.

Michael Day, **Modern art in English churches,** Mowbrays, 1984.

Tom Harrison, **Living through the Blitz,** Collins, 1976.

John Harvey, **English mediaeval architects. A biographical dictionary,** Sutton, 1984.

John Harvey, **The Perpendicular style, 1339–1485,** Batsford, 1978.

John Hayes, **The art of Graham Sutherland,** Phaidon, 1980.

A history of Staffordshire, v. 3, 1970 (VCH).

A history of Warwickshire, v. 2, 1908 (VCH).

Simon Houfe, **Sir Albert Richardson, the Professor,** White Crescent Press, 1980.

Edward D. Mills, **The modern church,** Architectural Press, 1956.

F. Moyle, **Neville Gorton,** SPCK, 1957 (Ch. 6, Spence on Gorton).

Nikolaus Pevsner and Alexandra Wedgwood, **Warwickshire,** Penguin, 1966.

Nikolaus Pevsner and Priscilla Metcalf, **The cathedrals of England. Midland, Eastern and Northern counties,** Viking, 1985.

Charles Phythian-Adams, **Desolation of a city. Coventry and the urban crisis of the Late Middle Ages,** Cambridge University Press, 1979.

The ruined St Michael's Cathedral Coventry (Coventry Cathedral, ND (mid-1980s)).

G. Kidder Smith, **The new churches of Europe,** Architectural Press, 1964, p.38–42.

Frederick Smith, **Coventry. Six hundred years of municipal life,** Corporation of the City of Coventry, November 1945.

Basil Spence and Henk Snoek, **Out of the ashes,** Bles, 1963. (Essay: Lewis Mumford).

Malcolm Yorke, **Eric Gill, man of flesh and spirit,** Constable, 1981.

PRINCIPAL PERIODICAL ARTICLES, REPORTS, & MISCELLANY

Building News, 31 October 1884; 14 November 1884 (tower restoration).

The Builder, 20 June 1891, p. 490–1 (proposed capanile).

M. D. Harris, **Transac. Birmingham Archae. Soc.,** 1927–8, p. 246–6 (misericords).

P. B. Chatwin, **Transac. Birmingham Archae. Soc.,** 1928, p. 132–144 (St Michael's).

Coventry Cathedral Chronicle, No. 2, 1936–7 (St Michael's new sanctuary).

Architects Journal, 17 February 1944, p. 137–8 (Giles Scott scheme).

The Builder, 17 January 1947, p. 73 (Scott resigns).

The Builder, 3 November 1950, p. 431 (competition details).

N. Pevsner, **Architectural Review,** January 1951, p. 3–6 ("Canons of Criticism").

Architects Journal, 23 August 1951, p. 217–224 (winning design, & others).

Architectural Design, September 1951, p. 257–264 (winning design, & others).

J. M. Richards, **Architectural Review,** January 1952, p. 3–7 (Spence design appraised).

RIBA Journal, December 1958, p. 46–9 (Spence address as President of RIBA).

The Observer, 14 June 1959 (detailed profile of Spence).

Sunday Times Colour Section, 20 May 1962 (Coventry Cathedral issue).

The Times, 25 May 1962 (Coventry Cathedral supplement; various contributions).

N. Pevsner, **The Guardian,** 25 May 1962, p. 6 (analysis of the cathedral).

Team Spirit, June 1962, Coventry Cathedral supplement (John Laing Group).

R. Furneaux Jordan, **Architectural Review,** July 1962, p. 24–34 (also 35–42).

Gilbert Cope, **The Listener,** 8 November 1962, p. 753–5 (broadcast transcript).

Anglican World, 1962, Coventry Cathedral feature (Bp. Bardsley, G. Cope).

Basil Minchin, **Church Building,** January 1963, p. 25–6 (**Phoenix** reviewed).

The Listener, 18 February 1965, p. 253–5 (transcript of interview of Spence).

The Times, 7 December 1967 (Spence resigns as Cathedral Architect).

Brian Hobley, 'Excavations at the Cathedral and Benedictine Priory of St Mary, Coventry' **Transac, Birmingham & Warwickshire Archaeological Soc.,** vol. 84 1971, p. 46–139. (Historical Survey by M. W. Lambert, and other contributions.)

H. Gordon Slade, **Archaeological Journal,** vol. 128, 1971, p. 252–3 (St Michael's).

RIBA Journal, January 1977 (Spence obituary by Richard Sheppard).

Martin Pawley, **Architects Journal,** 9 May 1984, p. 47–53 ("Building Revisits": 1).

Arup Journal, Spring 1985, p. 22 (Arup's article from The Times, 25 May 1962).

Edward D. Mills, article on Basil Spence in **Contemporary architects,** Muriel Emanuel, ed., Macmillan, 1980 (p. 768–9).

J. Thomas, **Church Building,** Christmas 1985, p. 36–8 (Giles Scott's design, etc.).

The new Coventry Cathedral plan and scheme, ND (1944). (Scott's cathedral.)

Coventry Cathedral. Report of Lord Harlech's commission, 10 June 1947, OUP, 1947.

Coventry Cathedral. Architectural competition conditions and instructions to competing architects, October 1950.

Coventry Cathedral. Architectural competition. Replies to questions, January 1951.

ACKNOWLEDGEMENTS

Many people have helped with the work, and in a variety of ways. At Coventry Cathedral I must thank the Provost, the Very Reverend Colin Semper, Richard Owen (Acting Archivist), Charles Brown (Cathedral Architect), Mr Timms (Head Verger), and other vergers and guides. Considerable assistance was given by the staffs of various libraries and collections: Coventry City Libraries, the British Architectural Library (RIBA), the Public Record Office, and others.

The following organizations loaned material for reproduction to illustrate this book: The Architectural Press (pp. 102, 103); the image on p. 27 is reproduced by permission of Birmingham and Warwickshire Archaeological Society from their Transactions 1971; Coventry City Libraries (pp. 54, 58, 62, 63, 65, 66); Coventry Record office (p. 28); the Royal Commission on the Historical Monuments of England (p. 90); and the British Architectural Library, RIBA, London (pp. 35 *left* 85, 95).

I must also thank Peter Burman, J. G. Davies, Robert Elwall, Liz Flintoff, Eric Hill (Lichfield Cathedral), Shirley Hind, Simon Houfe, Nigel Melhuish, Edward Mills, Martin Pawley, Richard Gilbert Scott, and A. Thorp (John Laing Construction Ltd.). Invaluable help with graphics was given by David Kitton (plans 1 & 3) and Stan Lody. I am also grateful to Chris Pickford (who helped in his capacity as County Archivist (Bedfordshire), and also made his detailed studies of St Michael's restoration and campanological arrangements available to me; hopefully, this work will be published before too long), and D. T. W. Price, who put his considerable knowledge of the Anglican Church and early British ecclesiastical history at my disposal. In all of my work, I am constantly indebted to Adrian Yardley, for his support, encouragement, and assistance; this project has been no exception. I must thank my wife Elaine, whose kitchen units will be fitted *one* day, and acknowledge the help and support of my friends and colleagues at South Bank Polytechnic. This book has been the product of teamwork, and I must thank Connie Austen-Smith and Barbara Fuller (Unwin Hyman), Harland Walshaw and Peter Burton, and Colin Lewis and Janet Tanner.

GLOSSARY

These definitions are not intended to be comprehensive but rather to indicate the senses in which the terms are used in this book.

AGORA A large open space for public assembly, surrounded by public buildings, as in Greek cities.

AISLE Volume of church or other building set parallel to the principal volume, divided off by columns, piers, etc., as in the BASILICAN arrangement. An open circulation space within a large space.

AMBO, AMBOS In modern usage, places from which the liturgy of the word is offered (pulpits, lecterns, etc.)

AMBULATORY A processional circulation space or aisle, generally around the back of the HIGH ALTAR, and semi-circular, polygonal or straight in plan. Often for pilgrims visiting saints' relics in a shrine.

ANGLE-BUTTRESS Buttress set against the corner of a structure.

APSE, APSIDAL A semi-circular or polygonal projection from the eastern or high altar end of a church, or Roman basilica, etc. Apsidal means apse-shaped or apse-like.

ARCADING, ARCADE A series of arches carried on columns (colonnade) or piers (or rising from the floor).

ARCHDEACONRY The territory administered by an Archdeacon, which is delegated to him by the diocesan bishop.

BALDACCHINO A canopy over an altar. Originally, this word referred to cloth canopies hung from the ceiling, but in more recent times (as with that at St Peter's Rome), the term has been used of canopies raised on columns (see CIBORIUM).

BAPTISTERY Building, or defined space within a church, where the Christian rite of initiation, baptism, is performed.

BAROQUE Art and architecture of the sixteenth and seventeenth centuries which used such devices as illusionism and manipulation of light to play on the emotions; such devices in art of other times are sometimes called baroque.

BASE The stone between a column's shaft and its plinth; the lowest course of masonry in a wall.

BASILICAN Of construction, basilican refers to a building of three volumes, subdivided into aisles by two rows of columns or piers which support a clerestory above. This was the form of the Roman civil basilica, and the early Christian churches derived from it. In the latter, the clergy sat in the APSE, at one end (where the governor had sat in the Roman version), and the altar was in front of him, the people beyond. This arrangement is known as the basilican plan.

BATTER A gradual inward inclination of a wall, in elevation, used to increase strength, or for aesthetic effect (battered towers look less gross when seen diagonally).

BAY Unit or compartment of a building in traditional architecture, subidivided by piers, columns, buttresses, etc.

BLIND TRACERY, BLIND ARCHES Tracery and arches within which there is solid stone, rather than apertures or openings.

BORED PILES Piles are foundation-posts set in the ground beneath buildings. Bored piles are cast in place with concrete being poured into holes drilled in the earth.

BUTTRESS Vertical masonry pier set against or within a wall to give support, or counter thrust of roof, arches, etc., above the wall.

CAMPANILE Tower holding a ring of bells. Generally set independently from the church (as is normal in Italy).

CANT, CANTED Set at an angle (other than 90°) in plan.

CANTORAL, CANTORIS The side of a cathedral choir where the cantor or precentor has his stall, ie. the north side.

CARTOON The sketch or painting used in the production of the final work.

CHANCEL The part of a church which houses a high altar (as PRESBYTERY, SANCTUARY), but *chancel* is often used to mean the whole eastern arm of a cruciform church.

CHARNEL HOUSE Place where human bones were deposited, after removal from the graveyard, the graves being used over again.

CHASE A slot or groove made in a wall, for the housing or keying-in of structural members, etc.

CHI-RHO The Greek letters with which the title *Christ* begins, set together in a monogram.

CHOIR, QUIRE The part of the church where services are sung and said, traditionally east of the crossing or screen.

CIBORIUM A canopy over an altar, supported by four columns, as in Early Christian, Baroque and modern usage. See also BALDACCHINO.

CIMENT FONDU A powdered high-alumina cement, composed of burnt limestone and bauxite; normally dark in colour, it hardens rapidly.

CLERESTORY The upper, open, stage or storey in the centre of an aisled structure. See also BASILICAN.

CONTRAPPOSTO A pose in which the upper part of the body is twisted in the opposite direction to the lower part.

COPE A liturgical vestment, derived from a Roman outdoor cloak, consisting of a semi-circular garment worn around the shoulders.

CROSIER The processional pastoral staff of a bishop, its termination shaped like a shepherd's crook.

CROSSING A central space where various volumes (nave, chancel, TRANSEPTS) of a church meet.

CRUCIFORM Cross-shaped, the normal plan for greater medieval churches. Any construction cross-shaped in plan.

CRYPT An underground chamber, beneath a church. In early times they were sometimes built to house saint's remains; in modern usage, the term is often used to mean undercroft or basement.

CUSPED TRACERY Tracery having points projecting inwards.

DECANAL, DECANIS The side of a cathedral choir where the dean has his stall, ie. the north side.

DWARF ARCADING Small set of arches on columns, normally non-structural, but part of internal decoration.

EXEDRA, EXEDRAE A portion of a building which projects externally from the main building, and often contains a chapel, baptistery, sacristy, etc. Used of projections whose nature and function is unknown.

EXTRADOS The outer (or upper) face of the stones that compose an arch (or vault).

FACADE The face or front of a building, the part intended to be looked at, often architecturally decorated.

FAN, FAN VAULT A feature of English Late Gothic architecture where concave semi-cones, meet, or almost meet, at the central ridge.

FLECHE A slender spire or spirelet, normally rising from the roof of a church, much used in French cathedrals. At Coventry, this form has been re-interpreted as a fine latticed mast-like structure.

FRIABILITY For stone, this means the material's innate tendency to break down and crumble due to weathering and/or chemical action.

GOTHIC ARCHITECTURE One of the great strands of western architecture, known by its use of pointed arches and vaults. It originated in the 1140s, and has existed in one form or other almost ever since.

GROIN VAULT A vault where two tunnel-vaults of the same shape intersect at right-angles.

HIGH ALTAR The principal altar (of many) in a medieval or Roman Catholic church; almost always set at the east end, it is the principal liturgical focus, which *High Altar* is sometimes used to mean, even when there are no others, and the altar is properly a Communion Table.

HYPERBOLIC PARABOLOID A surface whose extremities, on diagonal axes, are alternately raised and depressed; saddle-shaped.

INTAGLIO Forms cut into the surface of a material.

LATERAL AXIS In axially-planned buildings, this is the line running along the structure's length, and often along the users' line of sight. In cruciform churches, this means the nave and chancel's axis.

LIERNE VAULT Vault whose ribs include the *lierne* rib, a tertiary rib which neither joins the central boss nor springs from the columns.

LINTEL, LINTOL The horizontal beam at the top of door-frame or window-frame which supports the wall above the opening.

LOUVRES Slatted openings set in a window-arch or other opening for ventilation or the control of light.

MANDORLA Almond-shaped aureole or frame surrounding Christ (or the Virgin May), in depictions of the Ascension, Transfiguration, Assumption, or other settings (as in Sutherland's tapestry); same as *Vesica piscis*.

MANNERIST A term used for certain varieties of Italian art and artist of the years *c.* 1520–1600, between Renaissance and Baroque.

MARS The Modern Architecture Research group, composed of *avant garde* architects who furthered the cause of modern architecture in Britain, in the 1930s.

MASS CONCRETE Concrete without reinforcement.

MENSA The upper slab of an altar (*mensa* is Latin for 'Table').

MISERICORDS Brackets, often carved, set below an up-hinging seat, designed to support users during long services, as in a monastic choir (sometimes called *Misereres*).

MULLION A vertical post or member dividing windows, etc., into separate areas of glass (lights).

NAVE The central volume in the

BASILICAN system of building; the principal western volume of a traditional church, usually reserved for the laity.

NET-VAULT An Eastern European style of vault where the rib-work creates a continuous series of linked shapes (eg. lozenge) across the whole vault.

PANTOCRATOR, CHRIST An image of Christ as Ruler of All, often portrayed in the domes of Byzantine churches.

PARABOLIC ARCH, PARABOLOID An arch or curve having the shape of a circular cone cut vertically, or a length of chain hung from two level horizontal points (ie. catenary).

PIER A vertical supporting member of stone or other material, as also is a column; the former is generally square, the latter round, in plan.

PISCINA A basin with a drain, fixed to the wall beside the altar, where water used to clean sacred vessels is poured.

PLATE-TRACERY The earlier form of gothic tracery, where geometrical forms are cut through a slab of stone.

POLYESTER RESIN A variety of thermosetting plastic material (i.e. that which requires heat and pressure for forming, and does not soften on re-heating).

POST-MODERN, POST-MODERNISM A contemporary form of architecture which often presents quotations from the architectural vocabularies of the past, employs rampant eclecticism, and negates the ideas of structural logic and form based on function, of Modernism.

POST-TENSIONING A means of PRE-STRESSING concrete members by applying tension *after* the member is made (eg. by fixing taut steel cables within pre-cast concrete beams).

POST-TRIDENTINE After the Council of Trent (1545–63), ie. of the Counter-Reformation.

PRO-CATHEDRAL A church (normally a parish church) designated as a future cathedral.

PRESBYTERY The part of the church,

traditionally at the east, where the high altar is situated. This term is often used in a medieval monastic connection, and SANCTUARY in a modern Anglican connection.

PRE-STRESSING Applying forces to a structure (eg. of concrete) in order to strengthen it against structural loads.

PULPITUM A large stone screen, with gallery, dividing choir from nave; a more substantial version of a ROOD-SCREEN.

QUADRIPARTITE VAULT A vault where each bay is divided into four parts.

RAKED A horizontal surface which rises at one end, like a cinema floor.

REINFORCED CONCRETE Concrete containing steel rods or mesh which strengthens the material by resisting tensile stresses.

RENDERING Application of a coat of coarse plaster to a wall.

REREDOS A large panel behind and above an eastern altar. In English gothic, it is normally composed of decorative stonework and statuary. Continental churches often have an altarpiece, with a large central painted panel, in place of the reredos.

RETICULATIONS Forms which fill up an arch or window, producing a net-like effect.

RIB The structural and/or decorative member that subdivides the cells of a gothic vault.

RIB VAULT A vault supported by diagonally arched ribs.

ROOD SCREEN One of many kinds of screen which subdivided the liturgical areas of a medieval church, and people and their functions. This one held a rood (normally images of Christ on the Cross, with Mary and St John either side of him) on top of it.

RURAL DEANERY A group of parishes (not necessarily in the country) within a diocese.

SACRISTY A space attached to a church to hold sacred vessels, vestments, etc.

SANCTUARY The area containing the altar (see also PRESBYTERY, CHANCEL).

SCABBLING Rough dressing of stone with a sharp-pointed hammer.

SCREEN See ROOD-SCREEN, PULPITUM.

SILL The lower horizontal member of window or door openings, or framed structure.

SPALLING The splitting and crumbling of stonework.

SPANDREL, SPANDREL PANEL The flat triangular space between the arches of an arcade set in a straight line.

STRING-COURSE A projecting horizontal moulding running along a wall.

SUFFRAGAN BISHOP An assistant to the diocesan bishop, in whose diocese he works.

TIE-BEAM The lowest, horizontal, members of a truss.

TRANSEPT Transverse volumes of a medieval church, normally running north-south from the crossing, or from the western- or eastern-most bays of NAVE or CHANCEL.

TRANSOM A horizontal member, subdividing a window or panel.

TRANSVERSE AXIS The axis in a building which runs across the LATERAL AXIS, which, in a traditional church is north-south (eg. the TRANSEPTS).

VERMICULATION From the Latin for "worm", this is a form of stone decoration, used in Classical architecture, where the tracks of worms in wood are imitated.

WEATHERINGS Sloping horizontal surfaces found at ascending intervals on many gothic BUTTRESSES, designed to throw the rain off.

WEB, WEBBING In gothic vaults, the panels of stones between the ribs.

WEST FRONT The façade of the termination opposite the high altar in a medieval church, usually a screen decorated with statuary, etc., in English gothic architecture.

INDEX

Bold numerals refer to captions or illustrations

Aberdeen, David 94
Aidan, St 10
Aktion Sühnezeichen 116, 123
St Albans Cathedral 40
Albi Cathedral 95,127
Allen, W Godfrey 80
Altars, position of 83–5, 161–2, 163, 165, 166, 174
Anderson, Rowand 96
Archer, Thomas 41
Architects Journal 105
Architectural Design 172
Architectural Review 93, 104
Arden, deanery of 39
Arup, Ove 108, 122, 136, 138
St Asaph Cathedral 38
Augustine of Canterbury, St 10
Augustinians 15
Bablake School, Coventry 48
Baedeker raids 78, 80
Bagenal, Hope 150
Bardsley, Bishop Cuthbert K N 110–11, 114, 127
Bartning, O 92
Bath & Wells, diocese of 16, 22
'Battle of the Styles' 81, 82
Beckett, Archbishop Thomas à of Canterbury 18
Benedictines 11, 15, 18, 36, 38
Bentley, J F 83, 115
Bernini, G L 151
Beyer, Ralph 113, 116, 129, 140, **146**, 147
Birmingham Cathedral of St Chad 21
diocese and cathedral of St Philip 40, 41, 43
Bishop's Palace, Coventry 23, 31, 125
Bishoprics of Bradford and Coventry Act 1918 42
Black Death 18, 32
Blacking, W H Randoll 67, 70
Bliss, Sir Arthur 150
Blue Coat School, Coventry 28
Blythe, Bishop 21
Bond's Hospital 48
Booth, Bishop William 20
Botoner family 49
Bowlby, Dr 40
Bridge, Rev. A C 165
Bridgeman, John 155, **155**
Bridgeman, Mary 124
Britten, Sir Benjamin 150
War Requiem 150–1
Broadgate, Coventry 12, **13**
Brown, Caroline 140

Builder, The 87, 88, 89
Bullock, Sir Ernest 150
Burghill, Bishop John 49
Burton monastery 12
Butler, Bishop 39
Butter, Rev. J 62
Cachemaille-Day, N F 172–3
Camswell, Prior Thomas 21
Canterbury Cathedral 35, 38, 80
Cappers' Room 109, 123
see also guilds
Carlisle Cathedral 38, 62, 111
Carthusian priory, Coventry 20
Cathays Park, Cardiff 91
Cathedra (bishop's throne) 8, 11, 16
of new cathedral 148, 152
Cathedral competition 91–5
Cathedral Measures, the 43
Central Council for the Care of Churches 81, 109
St Chad, Bishop 8, **9**, 15, 18, 21
Catholic cathedral of, Birmingham 21
Chamberlain, Joseph 41
Chapter Houses 18, 38, 41, 129, 132, 179
Charles I 23, 48
Charles II 24
Chatwin, J A 41
Chatwin, P B 53, 109, 182
Chelmsford Cathedral 42
Chester 11
Abbey 35, 38
Cathedral 62
Earl of 15, 29
Earl Hugh of 44
Earl Ranulph of 44
Chevet 33–4
Cheylesmore, manor of 15
Christian Service Centre 83, 84, 86, 92, 166
Cistercians 15
City Hall, Coventry 47, 154
Civil War 23
Clement, Chapel of St, St Mary's 32
Churchill, Winston 68, 69
Clarke, Geoffrey 112, 116, 122, 131, 148, 152, 153, 154
Clifton Cathedral 6, 111, 162
Clitheroe, Graham 71, 72, 88
Close, Bishop Nicholas 20
Collegiate churches 16, 21
Comper, J N 83, 88
Cope, Dr Gilbert 163, 165
Coper, Hans 116, 152, **153**
Corbusier, Le 96, 173–4
Cornhull, Bishop de 17

Council of the Marches and Wales 20
Coventry Cathedral Act 1953 110
Coventry Cross 23
Coventry, deanery after 1836 39
Coventry Leet Book 26, 35
The court Leet 47–8
Coventry, modern churches by Basil Spence 173
Coventry, wartime destruction 68–9, 73–4, **75, 76**
Coventry, Walter of 26
Cromwell, Thomas 21, 22
Crosby, Prior Richard 20
'Cross of St Chad' 133
Cross, Chapel of the 51, **51**, 111, 131, 148
Cross, Charred 78, **79**, 92, 99, 120, 133, 159, 180
Cross of Nails 78, 92, 99, 133, 148, **150**, 158, 159
Community of 78, 168
Clinton, Bishop Roger de 133
Cuneo, Terence 159
Cuttoli, Marie 113
Dark, Frankland 116
Darwin, Robin 112
Davies, J G 166–8
Day, Michael 170, 182
Dick, Sir William Reid 12, **13**
Dissolution of the monasteries 11, 16, 21, 22, 26, 44
see also Succession, Act of
Supremacy, Act of
Douglas, Fr C E 107
Drayton-Wyatt, J 62, 63
Duck-Cohen, E 94
Dugdale, Sir William 27, 32, 51
Antiquities of Warwickshire 27
Monasticon Anglicanum 27
Dugdale, W S 40
Duncan, Perry 96
Dunstable, Prior William de 18
Durham Cathedral 126
Dwelly, F W, dean of Liverpool 84
Dyer's Chapel **45**, 59, 124
Earl's Half 15, 44, 50
Eccleshall Castle 20, 23
Ecclesiastical Commission 25, 39
Edmonds, Harry 156
Edmundsbury, St Cathedral 42, 178
Edric the Dane 12
Edward IV 20
Edward VI 22

Elizabeth I 22, 23
Elizabeth II 110
Embassy Chancery, Rome 100
Epstein, Sir Jacob 31, 113, 114, 115, 170, 172
door handles **129**, 129–30
Ecce Homo 123, **177**
Lucifer, Birmingham 113, 127
Madonna and Child, London 113
Majestas, Llandaff 113
St Michael and the Devil 31, 113, 114, 115, **125**, **126**, 127 169
Erith, Raymond 93, 94–5, 102
Esher, Lord 81
report 81
Established Church Act 1836 25
Exeter Cathedral 80
Festival of Britain 96, 100, 105, 168, 172
First Cathedral, see St Mary's, Priory Church of
First Diocese of Coventry 8–25
Fisher, Archbishop 84
Fitzgerald, Clarke 151
Forbes, 'Jock' 70, 78
Ford, E H 91
Ford's Hospital 48, 71
Forseth, Elinar **115**, 115–16, 156, 158, **159**
Frink, Elisabeth 116, **147**, 148, 152, 172
Frewen, Bishop Accepted 23, 39
Gaudi, A 173
Gee, David 124
Gibbord, Frederick 161 2
Gibson, Donald 81, 88
Gill, Eric 83, 162, 169
Gloucester Cathedral 22, 57, 126, 145
Gargano, Monte 50
Glastonbury Tor 50
Godiva or Godgyfu 11–13, 15, 21, 29, 31, 34, 161
Gore, Bishop Charles 40–1
Gorton, Bishop Neville C 82–4, 86, 89, 99, 106, 107, 110, 113, 124, 138, 150, 163, 166, 173
Gothic Revival 27, 175
Gott, Arthur 89
Grace, John 21
Green, Curtis 93
Gregory IX, Pope 44
Greyfriars Church **14**, **19**, 20, 26, **27**, 72, 122
'Griblock' 96
see Spence, Sir Basil
Guildford Cathedral 6, 7, 81, 91, 112, 161, 169
competition 81, 104
Guilds 46–9
Abolition of religious guilds 61

guild chapels 57, 59, 71, 151
Hacket, Bishop John 24
Haigh, Bishop M G 43, 82
memorial Chapel 50, 91, 123, 124
Hallowing Places 91, 92, 106, 123
Hammond, Peter 161, 162, 174–5
Hampton Lucy rectory 70
Harlech, Lord 87, 91, 99
Commission 43, 87–8
Harvey, John 57, 121, 182
Hearn, Albert 87
Hellberg, Rolf 94
Henry III 31, 37
Henry VI 20
Henry VII 20
Henry VIII 21, 22
Herbert Museum and Art Gallery, Coventry 29, 124, 144, 158
Hereford diocese 10, 16
Higgens, Archdeacon 23
Hitler, Adolf 68, 70
Hobley, Brian 29, 183
Holland, S 95
Holy Trinity Church, Coventry **13**, **14**, 15, 26, **27**, 28, 35, 44, 50, 61, 76, 78, 80, 87–8, 91, 110, 122, 133, 163
contrast with St Michael's 55, 57
wartime bombing 71, 72, 78
Honorius, Pope 44
Houfe, E A 95
House of Commons destroyed 80
restored 86, 93
Howard, Provost Richard Thomas 43, 70, 70, 80–1, 83–6, 89, 99, 107, 111–14, 120, 140, 141, 142, 160, 170, 182
Hussey, Dean Walter 168
Hutton, John **9**, 112–13, 137–8, **139**, **165**, 169
see also St Michael's—modern cathedral screen wall
Institute for the Study of Worship and Religious Architecture 162, 166
Irreys, Prior William 18, 32
Isabella, Queen 15, 18, 48
Jennings, Helen 156–7
St John the Baptist Church, Bablake, Coventry 48, 122
John of Gaunt 60
Jordan, R Furneaux 175, 176, 179, 183
Kampfgruppe 100 69
Kenilworth Castle 60
King's College, Cambridge Chapel 20
Knickebein system 69
Knox, E A 40–1
Laing, Sir John 110–11

Laing, J Construction Company 116
Lee, Laurence 112, 153, 154
Lee, Bishop Dr Rowland 21
Lees, F G 94
Leicester dioceses 10, 11, 43
provost of 87
Leigh, Lord 40
Leofric, Earl of Mercia 11, 12, 15, 21, 29
Leofwin, Bishop 11
Lichfield Cathedral 6, 8–25, 8, **9**, 10, 16, 17, 18, 21, 23, **24**, 34, 38, 57, 62, 129
Lichfield diocese 6, 8–25, 39–40, 129, 161
Lincoln Cathedral diocese 10, 16, 25, 37, 69, 137
Lindisfarne Abbey 10
Lisle Carr, Bishop C 42–3, 159
Liverpool Anglican Cathedral 6, 7, 41, 80–1, 82, 89, 104, 162, 168, 169
Liverpool Metropolitan Cathedral 7, 111, 144, 162, 174
Llandaff Cathedral 80, 113
Lollards 20–1
London, Dr 21
London, Synod of 11
Lutyens, Sir Edwin 96, 162, 174
Lutyens, Robert 93, 176
Lymesey, Bishop Robert de 11, 15, 17, 29, 34, 161
McGilley, Frank 122
Magdalen College, Oxford 23
Maguire, R 102
Malmesbury Abbey 37
Malmesbury, William of 26
Manchester, diocese of 25, 40, 41
Margaret, Queen 20
Marmion, Robert 29
MARS group 174
Marton, deanery of 39
St Mary's, Warwick 60, 80
St Mary's, Priory Church, Coventry Cathedral 11, 12, 15, 18, 21, 26–38, **27**, **30**, **33**, **35**, **36**, 46, 110, 132, 133–5
building campaigns and construction 29–34
St Mary's Episcopalian Cathedral, Edinburgh 89
St Mary's Hall, Coventry 47, 78
Mary, Queen 22–3
Mass Observation 73
Maufe, Sir Edward 82, 91–2, 94, 109, 112, 169, 172
Melbourne, Lord 25
Melville, Robert 148
Mercer's Chapel 59, 73, 123

Mercia, diocese of 6, 10, 15
St Michael's, Coventry
  second cathedral 23, 34,
  35, 38, 42–67, **45**, **51**, **54**,
  56, **58**, **62**, **63**, **64**, **65**,
  66, **75**, **77**
  Altar of Rubble, Altar of
  Reconciliation 78, **79**, 92,
  99, 101, 120
  apse 124, 129
  crypts **51**, 130–1, 136,
  166
  items rescued from
  burning cathedral 71–2,
  160
  lady chapel 50–1, 53, 72
  nave 52–3, 59–60
  presbytery (sanctuary) 57
  ruins as part of tour **75**,
  119–24, **167**, **171**, **177**
  symbolism of ruins 74–8,
  120, 170
  tower and spire **13**, **14**,
  51–2, **56**, 60, **62**, **63**, **64**,
  65, 74, 121–2, **131**
St Michael's third cathedral
  (Spence's cathedral)
  altar
    development of idea
    83–5
    high altar cross 148,
    149, **150**, 151, 152,
    153, 154
    position of 83–5, 174
    of Rubble 92, 99, 101
  Baptistery 101, 102, 122,
  127, 135–6, 144–7, 153
    window 112, 113, 116,
    135, 144–5, 158,
    169, 170, 171
  Candlesticks, high altar
  152, **153**
  Choir stalls 148
  Christ the Servant see
  Industry, Chapel of
  Consecration 117
  Development of design
  104–8, **102**, **103**
  Flèche 116–17
  Floor **139**, 140
  Font 116, **145**, 145–7,
  170 see also Baptistery
    original design 106,
    146
  Foundation Stone 113
  Gethsemane Chapel **114**,
  115, 133, **134**, 151, 156,
  166
  Holograms, Visitors'
  Centre 160, 170
  Industry, Chapel of
  (Christ the Servant) 112,
  128, 129, 132, 133,
  151–2, 158, 165, 179
  International Centre (for
  Reconciliation) 116, 123,
  124
  Lady Chapel 107, 111,
  113, 132–3, **134**, 142,
  143, 144, **149**, **150**,
  155–6, **155**, 158
    altar 155, **155**
    screen 155, **155**

Lectern 116, **147**, 148,
172
Nave (interior) 135–7
  eastern nave aisle
  147–51
  west side 156
Nave (exterior) **33**, **101**,
127
Northern Wall 132–3, **134**
Organ 148, **149**, 151
Porch 99, 101, 106,
125–7, **125**
Pulpit 148
Sanctuary 148
Screen wall, glass 101,
106, 135–40, **139**, **165**,
167, 169, 180
Tablets of the Word 106,
113, 116, **146**, 147–8,
150, 151 see also
Hallowing Places
Tapestry 100, 106, 107,
112–13, 116, 135, 140–4,
141, **142**, **143**, 155–6,
155, 163, 168, 169, 170
Unity, Chapel of 70, 83,
86, 87, 95, 101, 112,
122, 129, **130**, **131**, 132,
136, 144, 156–8, **157**,
159, 165, 166
  mosaic 116, 158, **159**
Vault 100, **102**, **103**, **105**,
106–7, 136–7
Visitors' Centre **131**, 132,
144, 156, 158–60, 166,
170, 180
Windows
  baptistery see
  baptistery, window
  Chapel of Unity
  114–15, 157, **157**
  Nave, saw toothed 100,
  101, 105, 127, 129,
  147, 152–4, 156, 171
  Swedish **115**, 115–16,
  156, 158, 166
  old glass 70, 158–9
Mills, Edward 174, 178,
182, 183
Minchin, Basil 163, 165,
183
Mirror, Daily 75
Misericords
  of St Michael's 60, 70,
  72, 182
Modern Movement in
architecture 82, 93, 169,
173, 174, 176
Moore, Henry 138, 140
Moore, Temple L 125
Morris, Sir Philip 87
Morris, William 86, 176
Morton, Provost C E 43,
159
Moser 92
Moyle, F 107, 182
Moyses, Prior 27, 29, 31,
34
Murray, James 62, 67
Murray, K 162
Muschamp, Bishop de 44
Mystery plays 48–9
New, Keith 112, 153, 154

New Foundation, cathedrals
of the 22
Nicholson, Sir Charles 81
Norbury, Roger 26
Norton, Sir Thomas 24
Norwich Cathedral 37
Nunant, Bishop Hugh de
17, 31, 44
St Osburg, Abbess of 12,
18, 49, 161
St Osburg, nunnery of 12,
29
St Osburg 18, 49, 161
St Osburg, shrine of 34, 37
Otto, Rudolph 98, 167
Owen, Wilfred 150
Oxford Cathedral 22, 25
Palmerston, Lord 40
Parliaments at St Mary's 18,
32
St Paul's Cathedral 57, 80
St Paul, Bow Common 162
Patey, Edward 178
Pawley, Martin 170, 180,
183
Pearson, J L 115
Peel, Robert 25
'Peeping Tom' 13
Penkridge, Staffordshire 16
Perkins, Rev. E Benson 87
Perowne, Bishop J J S 40
Perret, A 92
Peter, Bishop 11
Peterborough Cathedral 22,
37, 38
Pevsner, Nikolaus 7, 53–4,
93–4, 104, 113, 121, 138,
144, 174, 175, 179
Phillipson, W Oliver 174
St Philips, Birmingham
(Birmingham Cathedral)
40, 41
Philpott, Dr Henry, Bishop
40
Phoenix at Coventry (Basil
Spence) 96, 98, 102,
104, 108, 163, 173, 182
Pinckney, Roger 89
Pinton Frères 113
Piper, John 113, 116,
144–5
  painting in Herbert Art
  Gallery 144
Pollock, J 172
Porta Pia, Rome 101
Portsmouth Cathedral 43
Post-Modernism 162, 178
Potter, Joseph 61, 63
Prior's Half, Coventry 15,
18, 35, 44
Priory Row, Coventry **131**,
132–5, 158
Pro-cathedral, Coventry 41
Pucelle, Bishop 17, 44
Pugin, A W W 178
Puritans 13, 23, 61
Ramsden, Omar 159
Ratcliffe, Harold 127
Reconstruction Committee
91, 105, 107, 112, 113,
172
Reformation 22
  see also Dissolution

Repton, Derbyshire 15
Reynolds, Humphrey 21
Reyntiens, Patrick 113, 116, 144
  see also St Michael's cathedral—modern cathedral baptistery window
RFAC (Royal Fine Art Commission) 86, 87, 88, 109
RIBA (Royal Institute of British Architects) 82, 87, 88, 91, 92, 108
Ribbentrop, von 68
Richards, J M 104, 105, 175, 176
Richardson, Prof. Albert 81, 95
Ripon, diocese of 25
Robertson, Howard 91, 172
Rope, W F 108
Ross, Clifford 140
Roundheads 23
Runnymede, air force memorial 112
Ruskin, J 175
Russell, Gordon 140
Russell, R D 140
Ryder, Bishop Henry 25
Salisbury Cathedral 37
Samwell, Mrs Eliza 124
Saunders, Laurence 22
Schwartz, R 92
Scott, Sir George Gilbert 61, 80, 176
Scott, Sir Giles Gilbert 80–6, 85, 87, 88, 89, 93, 99, 104, 163, 168, 175
Scott, John Oldrid 62–6, 63, 64, 65, 72, 80, 121, 122, 176
Seaxwulf, Bishop 10–11
Second diocese of Coventry 39–43
Severa, Jindrich 147
Sharp, Thomas 27
Sheffield, diocese 42
Shell Centre, London 91
Sherborne Abbey, Dorset 57
Short, Ernest 172
Shrewsbury 22
Skillyngton (Skelyngton), Robert 60
Slade, H Gordon 180, 183

Smith, Bishop William 20
Smithson, Alison and Peter 94, 95, 174
Sonck, L 92
Southwark, Anglican diocese 41
Spence, Basil 95–117, 97, 120, 123, 127, 140, 145–6, 150, 152, 154, 163, 168, 169, 170, 172, 173, 174, 176, 178, 179, 180
Spon Street, Coventry, historic buildings 48
Stafford 16, 20, 24
  Bishop of 87
Stalingrad Cathedral, icon from 131
Stavenby, Bishop de 17
Stoneleigh, deanory of 39
Suppression, Act of 1536 21
Supremacy, Act of, 1534 21
Sutherland, Graham 106, 112, 156, 158, 168, 170, 172
  see also St Michael's modern cathedral—tapestry
Swansea civic centre 91
Sykes, Steven 114, 115, 151
Tamworth, Staffordshire 16
Temple, Archbishop William 84
'Templo of Peace', Cardiff 91
Tewkesbury Abbey 22, 34
Thomas, Sir Percy 87, 91, 172
Thomas, Rodney (Arcon) 94
Thorneycroft, Sir Hamo 42, 124, 172
Thornton, John 61
Thurston, Captain N I 112, 182
Tickner, T F 28–9
Times, The 93
Tippett, Sir Michael 150
Traherne, Margaret 114–15, 157
  see also St Michael's modern cathedral windows
Troughton, Dr 28, 28, 36

Truro diocese and Cathedral 7, 40, 41, 82, 89, 115, 168, 169
Valor Ecclesiasticus, 1535 26
VE Day 91
Verlade, F X 173
Verney, Stephen 78
Voysey, C F A 173
Wakefield Cathedral 43
Wales, Rev. A P 78
Warde, Joan 21
Watkin, David 162
Waterhouse, Michael 91
Webster, George 91
Wells Cathedral 34, 57, 137
  see also Bath & Wells diocese of
Wells, Randall 173
St Werburgh's monastery, Chester 22
Weseham, Bishop de 17, 44
Westminster 18
  Abbey 34, 35, 37, 176
  Cathedral 115, 168
Whistler, Laurence 93, 176
Whitby, Synod of 10
Whitefriars, Coventry 20
Williams, Provost Harold C N 111, 148, 154
Williams, Sheldon 148
Winchester Cathedral 37, 38
Woodcock, George 62, 66
Woodhouse, Frederic 6–7, 45, 63, 182
Woodward, Malcolm 160
Worcester, diocese and Cathedral 10, 16, 25, 39, 40, 41, 62
  Bishop of 20, 41
Wren, Sir Christopher 80
Wright, Laurence 105
Wulfric Spot 12
Wyatt, James 61
Wycliffe, John 20
Wyley Chapel 51, 51, 131–2
Wymondham, Norfolk 22
Wynford, Prior 21
Yeatman-Biggs, Bishop H W 41–3, 42, 124, 127, 172
Yevele, Henry 176
York Minster 61, 98
Zimbabwe 98